70 CARIBBEAN RECIPES

70 CARIBBEAN RECIPES

TASTE SENSATIONS FROM THE TROPICS

Deliciously authentic dishes from the islands of Jamaica, Cuba, Puerto Rico and the Bahamas, all shown step by step in 275 photographs

Rosamund Grant

HERMES HOUSE

This edition is published by Hermes House, an imprint of Anness Publishing Ltd
Hermes House, 88–89 Blackfriars Road, London SE1 8HA; tel. 020 7401 2077; fax 020 7633 9499

www.hermeshouse.com; www.annesspublishing.com

If you like the images in this book and would like to investigate using them for publishing, promotions
or advertising, please visit our website www.practicalpictures.com for more information.

Publisher: Joanna Lorenz
Editorial Director: Judith Simons
Editors: Clare Gooden and Molly Perham
Photographers: Nicki Dowey, Will Heap and Patrick McLeavey
Additional picture material provided by South American Pictures: pages 7–9
Home Economists: Fergal Connolly, Joanne Craig, Tonia George and Lucy McKelvie
Designer: Nigel Partridge
Production Manager: Steve Lang
Editorial Readers: Penelope Goodare and Jay Thundercliffe

ETHICAL TRADING POLICY

At Anness Publishing we believe that business should be conducted in an ethical and ecologically sustainable way, with respect
for the environment and a proper regard to the replacement of the natural resources we employ.
As a publisher, we use a lot of wood pulp in high-quality paper for printing, and that wood commonly comes from spruce trees.
We are therefore currently growing more than 750,000 trees in three Scottish forest plantations: Berrymoss (130 hectares/320 acres),
West Touxhill (125 hectares/305 acres) and Deveron Forest (75 hectares/185 acres). The forests we manage contain more than
3.5 times the number of trees employed each year in making paper for the books we manufacture.
Because of this ongoing ecological investment programme, you, as our customer, can have the pleasure and reassurance of knowing
that a tree is being cultivated on your behalf to naturally replace the materials used to make the book you are holding. For further
information about this scheme, go to www.annesspublishing.com/trees

A CIP catalogue record for this book is available from the British Library.

Previously published as *Taste of the Caribbean*

NOTES

For all recipes, quantities are given in both metric and imperial measures and, where appropriate, in standard cups and spoons.
Follow one set of measures, but not a mixture, because they are not interchangeable.

Standard spoon and cup measures are level. 1 tsp = 5ml, 1 tbsp = 15ml, 1 cup = 250ml/8fl oz

Australian standard tablespoons are 20ml. Australian readers should use 3 tsp in place of 1 tbsp
for measuring small quantities.

American pints are 16fl oz/2 cups. American readers should use 20fl oz/2.5 cups in place of 1 pint when measuring liquids.

Electric oven temperatures in this book are for conventional ovens. When using a fan oven, the temperature will probably
need to be reduced by about 10–20°C/20–40°F. Since ovens vary, you should check with your manufacturer's instruction
book for guidance.

Medium (US large) eggs are used unless otherwise stated.

Main front cover image shows barbecued jerk chicken – for recipe, see page 48.

PUBLISHER'S NOTE

Although the advice and information in this book are believed to be accurate and true at the time of going to press, neither the authors
nor the publisher can accept any legal responsibility or liability for any errors or omissions that may have been made nor for any
inaccuracies nor for any loss, harm or injury that comes about from following instructions or advice in this book.

CONTENTS

INTRODUCTION

A culinary cruise around the Caribbean is richly rewarding. Having feasted your eyes on beautiful turquoise sparkling seas, palm-fringed beaches, green velvet mountains and exquisite gardens, you can dine on dishes that are as diverse as the islands themselves. These islands offer some of the best seafood in the world, plus fragrant stews, spicy side dishes, unusual salads and sweet treats such as coconut ice cream and Caribbean fruit and rum cake.

EARLY HISTORY

The earliest inhabitants of the Caribbean islands were the Ciboney, hunter-gatherers who had themselves migrated from northern South America. They were supplanted by the Taino, Arawak-speaking fishermen and farmers, who in turn were harried by the warlike

Below: The Caribbean islands have a vast coastline and fish and shellfish play an enormous role in their cuisine.

Caribs in a pattern that would be repeated again and again down the centuries as nation after nation fought for control of the islands.

The Taino were peace-loving people who lived in small communities and grew cassava, corn, squash, (bell) peppers, beans, sweet potatoes and yams – crops that remain the mainstay of the Latin American diet. Those who lived on the coast caught fish, which they often ate raw, and their diet was supplemented with ducks, turtles, snakes and small rodents.

The arrival of Christopher Columbus in 1492 spelled the beginning of the end for the Taino. Many of them succumbed to diseases, such as measles and smallpox, never before seen on the islands. Others died in the service of Spanish settlers who worked them cruelly on the land and digging for gold. The Caribs fared a little better. Most of them were now confined to the more eastern islands, and their fierce

reputation and remote location acted as a deterrent to would-be settlers. However, by the end of the 16th century, only a handful of the former inhabitants of the islands remained.

In their place came Spanish, English, French and Dutch settlers, the latter occupying the islands that Christopher Columbus had overlooked: Aruba, Curaçao and Bonaire. These islands, which would eventually become part of the Dutch Antilles, were "discovered" in 1499 by Alonso de Ojeda, one of Amerigo Vespucci's henchmen, and settled first by the Spanish and then by Dutch traders in the first half of the 17th century. The British and French, meanwhile, were becoming solidly entrenched in the Caribbean. Having already taken St Christopher (St Kitts) in 1623, the British quickly set up colonies on the islands of Nevis, Barbados, Antigua and Montserrat, while the French settled in Guadeloupe, Martinique and St Lucia.

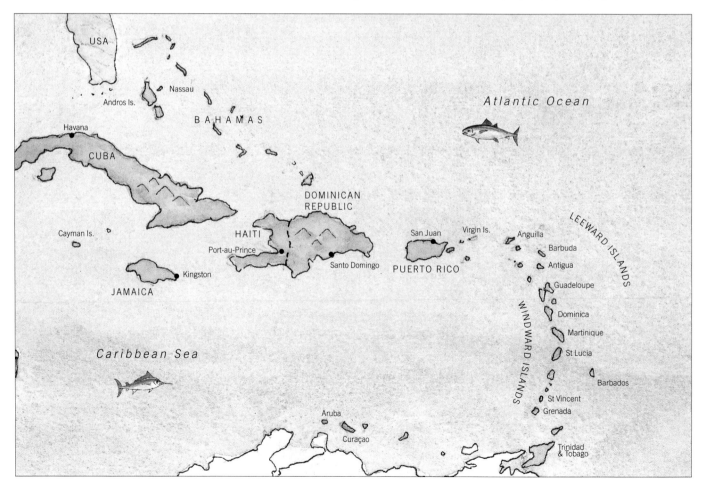

Above: A local woman inspects the produce at a street market.

SPANISH POSSESSIONS

The Spanish continued to dominate the most strategically important islands of Cuba, Jamaica, Puerto Rico and Hispaniola (modern day Haiti and the Dominican Republic).

During the next 200 years, the islands of the Caribbean became pawns in the hands of the European powers. They sometimes changed hands so frequently that would-be settlers set sail from home in the belief that they would be ruled by their compatriots, only to discover on reaching their destination that it was now under the control of someone else. The island of St Martin, for instance, was tossed between Holland, Great Britain and France more than a dozen times, the shortest period of occupation being just 10 days. The island is still half Dutch and half French, which explains why it is today known by two separate names: Sint Maarten and Saint Martin.

Today, most of the islands have achieved autonomy from their Euopean conquerors and have banded together to form Caricom, the Caribbean Community and Common Market.

FOOD AND DRINK

The turmoil of the early years meant that recipes were absorbed into the culture. The Spanish dish *pescado en escabeche* became known as eschovished fish, caveached fish or *escovitch*. *Callaloo*, a soup made from the leaves of a plant similar to spinach, is another successful migrant, being known variously as *le calalou, callilu, callau* and *calaloo*.

The French brought *bouillabaisse* to the islands, even though the fish used in the Caribbean version is very different from that found off the coast of Brittany. On Dominica and Montserrat they found frogs so large that their local name – mountain chicken – does not seem inappropriate. These French settlers wasted no time in teaching local cooks how to prepare frog's legs.

The Danes contributed recipes such as herring gundy, a dish of salt herring with potatoes, peppers and onion, and *croustadas*, which resemble savoury waffles. From the Dutch came *erwensoep* – a hearty pea soup – and the utterly delicious stew cooked within a whole cheese, *keshy yena*.

Made from fermented sugar cane, some of the world's best rums are still produced in the Caribbean, and rum cocktails are always a popular choice.

Below: Hard-working fishermen bring the daily catch ashore, ready to be sold at market.

Creole cooking

This term is used to describe many traditional Caribbean recipes. It generally refers to dishes that have their roots in both Europe and Africa, and is also used in Louisiana and some other southern states of the USA. There, Creole cooking has French, Spanish and African influences, whereas in the Caribbean, the Spanish and African influences are dominant. The expression *cocina criolla* is loosely applied throughout Latin America as a catch-all term for the native cuisine.

Above: Sugar cane is a major export for the region; the annual harvest in Cuba is exhausting but rewarding work.

NEW CROPS

It is widely believed that Columbus planted the first sugar cane on the Caribbean islands. By the start of the 17th century, the crop's huge potential was being fully appreciated, and large sugar cane plantations had been established, together with plantations of other crops new to the islands, such as bananas, plantains, coffee, coconuts and oranges.

Growing all of these new crops required a large amount of labour, and since the indigenous population had been largely wiped out, this led to the importation of slaves on a massive scale. They arrived in their thousands, enduring dreadful journeys by sea and harsh lives after reaching their destination. The slaves often had to subsist on dried fish or meat alone, since they were forbidden from raising cattle and denied the opportunity to catch fresh fish. The many traditional Caribbean dishes based on salt cod, such as Jamaican salt fish and ackee, originated during this period. The

slaves, who came mainly from West Africa, introduced ingredients such as yams and okra, which were quickly incorporated into the Caribbean cuisine. They improved their bland diet even further by the imaginative use of spices, laying the foundation for the hot pepper sauces that would become synonymous with the islands in years to come.

When slavery was eventually abolished in the 1830s, indentured labourers from the Middle East, India and the Far East were brought to the islands; these labourers introduced yet more ingredients to the melange that is Caribbean cooking. Spicy curries and dishes such as lamb pelau entered the repertoire, along with *roti* and *dhal puri*, large flat breads filled with curried meat, fish or potatoes.

Today it is mainly tourism that drives the economy of the Caribbean islands. Although this has had some negative effects on the local cuisine, mainly due to the introduction of the "international menu" that some travellers demand, it has also stimulated interest in regional specialities. The more dynamic Caribbean chefs are revelling in the wonderful ingredients that are at their disposal, especially the superb seafood on offer all year round. New and exciting dishes continue to emerge alongside old favourites.

STREET FOOD AND SNACKS

Snacking is a popular pastime on the Caribbean islands, which goes some way towards explaining the abundance of food available from roadside stalls and bars, or beach vendors. In fact, street food accounts for 20–30 per cent of urban household expenditure on the islands. Whatever the time of day, wherever you are, tasty morsels can be found to satisfy your hunger pangs.

Among the items traditionally offered by street vendors are deliciously light fritters, made from conch, salt cod or perhaps split peas, with spring onions (scallions) or chillies for extra flavour. Barbecued jerk chicken is another favourite, and for easy eating and instant gratification you cannot beat a bowl of crispy plantain and sweet potato chips or lightly cooked coconut king prawns, served with a glass of ice cold beer or one of the rum cocktails for which the islands are famous.

The quintessential Caribbean fast food, enjoyed by locals and tourists alike, is *roti,* a large flat bread with a tasty curried filling such as conch, goat or a selection of vegetables. Plantain dumplings are also a popular choice.

Below: In Havana, Cuba, a street vendor prepares sausages, delicious stuffed pastries and fried potatoes.

Above: The "Day of Kings" festival, which celebrates African gods, is a time for partying on the streets of Cuba.

FEASTS AND FESTIVALS

Carnival is the highlight of the year on the Caribbean islands. The build-up begins with the calypso season, which starts in January, then as Ash Wednesday approaches, signalling a period of sobriety and self-control, the streets ring to the sound of steel bands. In Aruba and Trinidad and Tobago, Carnival is a particularly extravagant affair. Local festivals are also held throughout the year. Puerto Rico commemorates the island's African-American heritage every June, and Jamaica has a popular reggae festival in July. Saints' days are always a good excuse for a celebration too, and they inevitably offer the opportunity to sample local food.

Special occasions are often marked by the roasting of a suckling pig. Slow roasting and regular basting ensures

that the meat is beautifully tender, but the best part for many diners is the stuffing. This varies from island to island and from cook to cook, often being made to a recipe that is a closely guarded secret. It may be hot and spicy, fresh and fruity or made from offal, with the heart, liver and kidneys of the pig mixed with sausage, onions and herbs. Rum or brandy is often added to give an extra kick.

No festival would be complete without food, and traditional Caribbean festival fare, available from street vendors, includes fish cakes, Jamaican salt fish fritters ("stamp and go") and rice and peas. More adventurous regional delicacies include *griot* (hot Haitian fried pork), jerked chicken and curried goat. Street-side food vendors can often be seen serving up more exotic foods, including fresh catfish and red snapper, Thai noodles or Mexican empanadas. In addition, hot dogs, sweets (candy), fresh fruit smoothies, soft drinks, ice-cold beer and rum cocktails are always popular.

The rum tradition
Not much goes on in the Caribbean that doesn't involve rum. It was developed in the 16th century by colonists who distilled molasses to trade for slaves in Africa. From here it was sent north to European markets, where a Spanish wine merchant, Facundo Bacardi, developed a process of charcoal filtering, to make rum taste better. Bacardi is now the leading brand of white rum and the best-selling spirit worldwide. Aged rum is darker, taking on the colour of the barrel in which it ages. It has a mellower taste that makes it perfect for sipping. Not all dark rums are aged, however – some have colour and flavour additives. There are dozens of rum cocktails available throughout the Caribbean. Three favourites are the daiquiri, the mojito and the pina colada.

Snacks and Soups

Throughout the Caribbean there is a tradition of street food. Market stalls, beach huts, bars and snack houses all offer sweet or savoury snacks, which make perfect accompaniments to fruit juice, cold beer or cocktails. The colonizers of the Caribbean introduced soup to the region, transforming their original recipes with the use of local ingredients.

PLANTAIN AND SWEET POTATO CHIPS

SALTY YET SWEET, THESE CRISP CHIPS ARE A CARIBBEAN SPECIALITY AND MAKE A DELICIOUS SNACK.

SERVES FOUR

INGREDIENTS
  2 green plantains
  1 small sweet potato
  oil, for deep-frying
  salt

VARIATIONS
For maximum crispness, it is important to use green plantains. If these are not available, substitute green bananas. Yam can be used instead of sweet potatoes. The vegetables must be soaked in cold salted water to prevent discoloration.

1 Using a small sharp knife, trim the plantains and cut them in half widthways. Peel by slitting the skin with a knife, following the natural ridges, then lifting it off. Place the peeled plantains in a bowl of cold, salted water.

2 Peel the sweet potato under cold running water, and add it to the plantains in the bowl.

3 Heat the oil in a large pan or deep-fryer. Remove the vegetables from the salted water, pat dry on kitchen paper and slice into thin rounds.

4 Fry the plantains and sweet potatoes in batches for about 2 minutes until crisp, then remove with a slotted spoon and drain on kitchen paper. Sprinkle with salt and serve when cool.

COCONUT KING PRAWNS

POPULAR THROUGHOUT THE CARIBBEAN ISLANDS, THESE BUTTERFLIED PRAWNS LOOK VERY PRETTY AND THEY TASTE WONDERFUL WHEN PARTNERED WITH A CRISP COCONUT AND CHIVE COATING.

SERVES FOUR

INGREDIENTS
  12 raw king prawns (jumbo shrimp)
  2 garlic cloves, crushed
  15ml/1 tbsp lemon juice
  50g/2oz/4 tbsp fine desiccated (dry unsweetened shredded) coconut
  25g/1oz/⅔ cup chopped fresh chives
  150ml/¼ pint/⅔ cup milk
  2 eggs, beaten
  salt and ground black pepper
  oil, for deep-frying
  lime or lemon wedges and fresh flat leaf parsley, to garnish

COOK'S TIP
If raw king prawns (jumbo shrimp) are difficult to obtain, substitute cooked prawns. However, the raw prawns will absorb more flavour from the marinade, so they are the ideal choice.

1 Peel and de-vein the prawns, leaving the tails intact, then deepen the incision made when de-veining the prawns, cutting from the back almost to the belly so that they can be opened out. Rinse the prawns under cold water and pat dry.

2 Mix the garlic and lemon juice with a little seasoning in a shallow dish, then add the prawns. Toss to coat, cover and marinate for about 1 hour.

3 Mix the coconut and chives in a separate shallow dish, and put the milk and eggs in two small bowls. Dip each prawn into the milk, then into the beaten egg and finally into the coconut and chive mixture.

4 Heat the oil in a large pan or deep-fryer and fry the prawns for about 1 minute, until golden. Lift out and drain on kitchen paper. Serve hot, garnished with lime or lemon wedges and parsley.

CHEESY EGGS

THESE TASTY CARIBBEAN STUFFED EGGS ARE SIMPLE TO MAKE AND IDEAL FOR LAST-MINUTE PARTY SNACKS. SERVE THEM WITH A CRISP SALAD GARNISH AND DHAL PURI.

SERVES SIX

INGREDIENTS

  6 eggs
  15ml/1 tbsp mayonnaise
  30ml/2 tbsp grated Cheddar cheese
  2.5ml/½ tsp ground white pepper
  10ml/2 tsp chopped fresh chives
  2 radishes, thinly sliced, to garnish
  lettuce leaves, to serve

VARIATION
A variety of fillings can be used instead of Cheddar cheese. Canned sardines or tuna mayonnaise make a tasty alternative.

1 Cook the eggs in boiling water for about 10 minutes until hard-boiled. Lift out the eggs and place them in cold water. When cool, remove the shells.

2 Put the mayonnaise, Cheddar cheese, pepper and chives into a small bowl. Cut the hard-boiled eggs in half lengthways and carefully scoop out the yolks without breaking the whites. Add the yolks to the bowl.

3 Mash all the ingredients with a fork until well blended.

4 Fill each egg white with the egg yolk and cheese mixture, and arrange on a plate. Garnish with thinly sliced radishes and serve with crisp green lettuce leaves.

CRAB CAKES

SERVED WITH A HOT AND SPICY TOMATO DIP, THESE CARIBBEAN CRAB CAKES ARE QUITE DELICIOUS. USE THE FRESHEST CRAB MEAT AVAILABLE AND SERVE AS A SNACK AT ANY TIME OF DAY.

MAKES ABOUT FIFTEEN

INGREDIENTS
    225g/8oz white crab meat
    115g/4oz cooked potatoes, mashed
    30ml/2 tbsp fresh herb seasoning
    2.5ml/½ tsp prepared mild mustard
    2.5ml/½ tsp ground black pepper
    ½ fresh hot chilli, seeded
        and chopped
    2.5ml/½ tsp dried oregano, crushed
    1 egg, beaten
    15ml/1 tbsp shrimp paste (optional)
    flour, for dusting
    oil, for frying
    lime wedges and fresh basil leaves,
        to garnish
For the tomato dip
    15ml/1 tbsp butter or margarine
    ½ onion, finely chopped
    2 canned plum tomatoes, drained
        and chopped
    1 garlic clove, crushed
    150ml/¼ pint/⅔ cup water
    5–10ml/1–2 tsp malt vinegar
    15ml/1 tbsp chopped fresh
        coriander (cilantro)
    ½ chilli, seeded and chopped

1 To make the crab cakes, combine the crab meat, mashed potato, herb seasoning, mustard, black pepper, chilli, oregano and egg in a large bowl. Add the shrimp paste, if using, and mix well. Cover and chill for 30 minutes.

VARIATION
If you cannot get hold of fresh crab meat, these taste just as good made with canned tuna.

2 Make the tomato dip. Melt the butter or margarine in a small pan. Add the onion, chopped tomato and garlic and sauté for about 5 minutes until the onion is soft.

3 Add the water, vinegar, coriander and chilli. Simmer for 10 minutes, then blend to a smooth purée in a food processor or blender. Pour into a bowl. Keep warm or chill, as required.

4 Using a spoon, shape the crab mixture into rounds and dust with flour. Heat a little oil in a large frying pan and fry the crab cakes, a few at a time, for 2–3 minutes on each side until golden brown. Remove with a fish slice, drain on kitchen paper and keep hot while cooking the remaining cakes. Serve with the tomato dip and garnish with lime wedges and basil leaves.

SPINACH PATTIES

THESE LITTLE SPINACH PIES, LIGHTLY SPICED WITH CUMIN, ARE JUST THE THING FOR A PICNIC LUNCH OR AS PART OF A BUFFET MEAL. THEY ARE EQUALLY GOOD SERVED HOT OR COLD.

SERVES FOUR TO SIX

INGREDIENTS
For the pastry
 115g/4oz/½ cup butter or margarine,
  chilled and diced
 250g/8oz/2 cups plain (all-purpose)
  flour
 1 egg yolk
 milk, to glaze
For the filling
 25g/1oz/2 tbsp butter or margarine
 1 small onion, finely chopped
 175g–225g/6–8oz fresh or frozen
  leaf spinach, chopped
 2.5ml/½ tsp ground cumin
 ½ vegetable stock cube, crumbled
 freshly ground black pepper

1 Preheat the oven to 200°C/400°F/ Gas 6. Lightly grease 10 or 12 muffin tins (pans).

2 To make the filling, melt the butter or margarine in a pan, add the onion and cook gently until softened. Stir in the spinach, add the cumin, stock cube and pepper and cook for 5 minutes or until the spinach has wilted. Leave to cool.

3 To make the pastry, rub the butter or margarine into the flour, add the egg yolk and 30–45ml/2–3 tbsp cold water and mix to a firm dough.

4 Turn the the pastry out on to a floured surface and knead for a few seconds. Divide the pastry in half and roll out one half. Cut out 10 or 12 rounds using a pastry cutter. Press into the muffin tins and fill with the spinach mixture.

5 Roll out the remaining dough and cut out smaller rounds to cover the patties. Press the edges to seal and prick the tops with a fork. Brush with milk and bake for 15–20 minutes until golden.

SALT FISH FRITTERS ("STAMP AND GO")

THESE DELICIOUS SALT FISH FRITTERS ARE ALSO KNOWN AS ACCRAS.

SERVES FOUR TO SIX

INGREDIENTS
 115g/4oz/1 cup self-raising (self-
  rising) flour
 115g/4oz/1 cup plain (all-purpose)
  flour
 2.5ml/½ tsp baking powder
 175g/6oz soaked salt cod, shredded
 1 egg, whisked
 15ml/1 tbsp chopped spring onions
  (scallions)
 1 garlic clove, crushed
 2.5ml/½ tsp ground black pepper
 ½ hot chilli pepper, seeded and
  finely chopped
 1.5ml/¼ tsp turmeric
 45ml/3 tbsp milk
 vegetable oil, for shallow frying

1 Sift the flours and baking powder together into a bowl, then add the salt cod, egg, spring onion, garlic, pepper, hot chilli pepper and turmeric. Add a little of the milk and mix well.

2 Gradually stir in the remaining milk, adding just enough to make a thick batter. Stir thoroughly and beat with a wooden spoon so that all the ingredients are completely combined.

3 Heat a little oil in a large frying pan until very hot. Add a few spoonfuls of the batter mixture and fry for a few minutes on each side until golden brown and puffy. Lift out the fritters with a slotted spoon, drain on kitchen paper and keep warm.

4 Cook the rest of the batter mixture in the same way. Serve the fritters hot or cold, as a snack.

FISH AND SWEET POTATO SOUP

THE SUBTLE SWEETNESS OF THE POTATO COMBINES WITH THE STRONGER FLAVOURS OF FISH AND OREGANO TO MAKE THIS AN APPETIZING SOUP, POPULAR THROUGHOUT THE CARIBBEAN.

SERVES FOUR

INGREDIENTS
175g/6oz white fish fillet, skinned
½ onion, chopped
1 sweet potato, about 175g/6oz,
  peeled and diced
1 small carrot, about 50g/2oz,
  chopped
5ml/1 tsp chopped fresh oregano or
  2.5ml/½ tsp dried oregano
2.5ml/½ tsp ground cinnamon
1.35 litres/2¼ pints/5½ cups
  fish stock
75ml/5 tbsp single (light) cream
chopped fresh parsley, to garnish

1 Remove any bones from the fish and put it in a pan. Add the onion, sweet potato, carrot, oregano, cinnamon and half of the stock. Bring to the boil, then simmer for 20 minutes or until the potatoes are cooked.

2 Leave to cool, then pour into a food processor and blend until smooth.

3 Return the soup to the pan, stir in the remaining fish stock and gently bring to the boil. Reduce the heat.

4 Stir the cream into the soup, then gently heat it through without boiling. If the soup boils the cream will curdle. Serve hot, garnished with the chopped parsley.

CARIBBEAN VEGETABLE SOUP

THIS HEARTY VEGETABLE SOUP IS FILLING ENOUGH TO BE SERVED ON ITS OWN FOR LUNCH, BUT STRIPS OF COOKED MEAT, POULTRY OR FISH CAN ALSO BE ADDED.

SERVES FOUR

INGREDIENTS
25g/1oz/2 tbsp butter or margarine
1 onion, chopped
1 garlic clove, crushed
2 carrots, sliced
1.5 litres/2½ pints/6¼ cups
  vegetable stock
2 bay leaves
2 fresh thyme sprigs
1 celery stick, finely chopped
2 green bananas, peeled
  and quartered
175g/6oz white yam or eddoe,
  peeled and cubed
25g/1oz/2 tbsp red lentils
1 chayote (christophene), peeled
  and chopped
25g/1oz/2 tbsp macaroni (optional)
salt and ground black pepper
chopped spring onion (scallion),
  to garnish

1 Melt the butter or margarine in a pan and fry the onion, garlic and carrots for a few minutes, stirring occasionally.

2 Add the stock, bay leaves and thyme, and bring to the boil.

3 Add the celery, green bananas, white yam or eddoe, lentils, chayote and macaroni, if using. Season with salt and ground black pepper and simmer for 25 minutes or until the vegetables are cooked through. Serve garnished with chopped spring onion.

VARIATION
Use other root vegetables, such as potatoes or sweet potatoes, if yam or eddoes are not available.

BEEF AND CASSAVA SOUP

THIS SIMPLE, TASTY SOUP IS ALMOST A STEW. SUCH SOUPS, MADE IN ONE POT, ARE EVERYDAY FARE IN THE CARIBBEAN. THE ADDITION OF WINE IS NOT TRADITIONAL, BUT IT ENHANCES THE FLAVOUR.

SERVES FOUR

INGREDIENTS

450g/1lb stewing beef, cubed
1.2 litres/2 pints/5 cups beef stock
300ml/½ pint/1¼ cups white wine
15ml/1 tbsp soft brown sugar
1 onion, finely chopped
1 bay leaf
1 bouquet garni
1 fresh thyme sprig
15ml/1 tbsp tomato purée (paste)
1 large carrot, sliced
275g/10oz cassava or yam, peeled
  and cubed
50g/2oz fresh spinach, chopped
a little hot pepper sauce, to taste
salt and ground black pepper

1 Mix the cubed beef, stock, white wine, sugar, chopped onion, bay leaf, bouquet garni, thyme and tomato purée in a large pan. Bring to the boil, then cover and simmer very gently for about 1¼ hours. If you want very tender meat, allow about 2–2¼ hours.

2 Add the sliced carrot, cubed cassava or yam, spinach and a few drops of hot pepper sauce. Season with salt and ground black pepper to taste and simmer for a further 15 minutes until the meat and vegetables are both tender. Serve in heated bowls.

LAMB AND LENTIL SOUP

LENTILS ARE POPULAR ON CARIBBEAN ISLANDS, SUCH AS TRINIDAD AND TOBAGO, WHERE THEY WERE INTRODUCED BY SOUTH-EAST ASIAN LABOURERS RECRUITED TO WORK THE SUGAR CANE PLANTATIONS.

SERVES FOUR

INGREDIENTS
　1.5–1.75 litres/2½–3 pints/
　　6¼–7½ cups water or stock
　900g/2lb neck of lamb, cut
　　into pieces
　½ onion, chopped
　1 garlic clove, crushed
　1 bay leaf
　1 clove
　2 fresh thyme sprigs
　225g/8oz potatoes
　175g/6oz/¾ cup red lentils
　600ml/1 pint/2½ cups water
　salt and ground black pepper
　chopped fresh parsley

1 Pour 1.5 litres/2½ pints/6¼ cups of the water or stock into a large pan and add the lamb, chopped onion, crushed garlic, bay leaf, clove and thyme sprigs. Bring to the boil, then lower the heat and simmer gently for about 1 hour, until the lamb is tender.

2 Peel the potatoes and cut them into rough 2.5cm/1in cubes. Add them to the soup in the pan and cook for a further 5 minutes.

3 Add the red lentils to the pan, stirring them gently into the stock, then season the soup to taste with a little salt and plenty of ground black pepper. Add approximately 300ml/½ pint/1¼ cups of warm water to completely cover the meat and vegetables.

4 Bring the soup back to the boil, then lower the heat, cover and simmer for 25 minutes or until the lentils are cooked, stirring occasionally. Add a little more water during cooking if the soup becomes too thick. Just before serving, stir in the chopped parsley.

CREAMY SPINACH SOUP

THIS APPETIZING SOUP HAS A LUXURIOUS, CREAMY, ALMOST VELVETY TEXTURE. THE SUBTLE TASTE OF COCONUT GIVES THE SPINACH A CARIBBEAN FLAVOUR. SERVE WITH CORN STICKS OR FRESH BREAD FOR A SATISFYING LUNCH – YOU WILL FIND YOURSELF MAKING IT OVER AND OVER AGAIN.

SERVES FOUR

INGREDIENTS
25g/1oz/2 tbsp butter
1 small onion, finely chopped
675g/1½lb fresh spinach, chopped
1.2 litres/2 pints/5 cups
  vegetable stock
50g/2oz creamed coconut
freshly grated nutmeg
300ml/½ pint/1¼ cups single
  (light) cream
salt and ground black pepper
fresh chopped chives, to garnish

1 Melt the butter in a large pan over a moderate heat. Add the onion and sauté for 3–4 minutes until soft.

2 Add the spinach, cover and cook gently for 10 minutes, until the spinach has reduced.

3 Pour the spinach mixture into a blender or food processor and add a little of the stock. Blend until smooth.

4 Return the mixture to the pan and add the remaining stock, creamed coconut, salt, pepper and nutmeg. Simmer for 15 minutes to thicken.

5 Add the cream, stir well and heat through, but do not boil. Serve hot, garnished with chives.

COOK'S TIP
If fresh spinach is not available, use frozen. Milk can be substituted for the cream – in which case, use half stock and half milk.

SPLIT PEA AND PUMPKIN SOUP

THIS CREAMY PEA SOUP IS ENLIVENED WITH CHUNKS OF PUMPKIN AND TOMATOES, WHICH GIVE IT TEXTURE, COLOUR AND FLAVOUR. IN THE CARIBBEAN, SALT BEEF IS OFTEN ADDED TO TURN THE SOUP INTO A COMPLETE MEAL.

SERVES SIX

INGREDIENTS
225g/8oz split peas, soaked
1.2 litres/2 pints/5 cups water
25g/1oz/2 tbsp butter or margarine
1 onion, finely chopped
225g/8oz pumpkin, chopped
3 fresh tomatoes, peeled and
   chopped
5ml/1 tsp dried tarragon, crushed
15ml/1 tbsp chopped fresh coriander
   (cilantro)
2.5ml/½ tsp ground cumin
vegetable stock cube, crumbled
chilli powder, to taste
coriander (cilantro) sprigs, to garnish

1 Soak the split peas overnight in enough water to cover, then drain.

2 Next day, place the split peas in a large pan, add the water and boil for about 30 minutes until cooked.

3 In a separate pan, melt the butter or margarine and sauté the onion for 4–5 minutes until soft but not browned.

4 Add the pumpkin, tomatoes, tarragon, coriander, cumin, vegetable stock cube and chilli powder and bring to the boil.

COOK'S TIP
Replace the unsalted peanuts with peanut butter, if you like. Use equal quantities of chunky and smooth peanut butter for the ideal texture.

5 Stir the vegetable mixture into the cooked split peas and their liquid. Simmer gently for 20 minutes or until the vegetables are tender. If the soup is too thick, add another 150ml/½ pint/ ⅔ cup water.

6 Spoon into warmed bowls and serve hot, garnished with coriander.

FISH AND SHELLFISH

With the numerous coastlines and a strong tradition of fishing, the people of the Caribbean have always enjoyed a wide variety of fresh fish and shellfish. Common fish include snapper, mahi mahi and grouper, but if you are unable to obtain these exotic fish, trout or filleted white fish make good substitutes. Prawns, crab, mussels and clams feature in many local recipes.

SALMON in MANGO and GINGER SAUCE

MANGO AND SALMON MAY SEEM UNLIKELY PARTNERS, BUT THE FLAVOURS COMPLEMENT EACH OTHER VERY WELL, ESPECIALLY WHEN THE DISTINCT FLAVOUR OF TARRAGON IS ADDED TO THE EQUATION.

SERVES TWO

INGREDIENTS

2 salmon steaks, each about
  275g/10oz
a little lemon juice
1–2 garlic cloves, crushed
5ml/1 tsp dried tarragon, crushed
2 shallots, roughly chopped
1 tomato, roughly chopped
1 large ripe mango, peeled, stoned
  (pitted) and chopped
150ml/¼ pint/⅔ cup fish stock
  or water
15ml/1 tbsp syrup from a jar of
  preserved ginger
25g/1oz/2 tbsp butter
salt and ground black pepper

1 Place the salmon steaks in a single layer in a shallow dish and sprinkle with the lemon juice, garlic, tarragon and salt and pepper. Cover and set aside in the refrigerator for at least 1 hour.

2 Meanwhile, place the shallots, tomato and mango in a blender or food processor and blend until smooth. Add the fish stock or water and the ginger syrup, blend again and set aside.

3 Melt the butter in a frying pan and cook the salmon steaks for about 3 minutes on each side.

4 Add the mango purée, cover and simmer for a further 5 minutes, until the salmon is cooked and flakes easily.

5 Transfer the salmon to plates. Heat the sauce, adjust the seasoning and pour over the salmon. Serve hot.

FRIED SNAPPER with AVOCADO

THE COMBINATION OF CRISP FRIED FISH AND SILKY SMOOTH AVOCADO WORKS EXTREMELY WELL IN THIS RECIPE. IN THE ISLANDS OF THE CARIBBEAN, WHERE THIS RECIPE ORIGINATED, THE FISH IS OFTEN SERVED WITH FRIED DUMPLINGS OR HARD-DOUGH BREAD.

SERVES FOUR

INGREDIENTS

1 lemon
4 red snappers, each about
  225g/8oz, prepared
10ml/2 tsp spice seasoning
flour, for dusting
oil, for frying
2 avocados and cooked corn, sliced
  widthways, to serve
chopped fresh parsley and lime
  slices, to garnish

1 Squeeze the lemon juice both inside and outside the fish, and sprinkle with the spice seasoning. Place the fish in a shallow dish, cover and set aside in a cool place to marinate for a few hours.

2 Lift the marinated fish out of the dish and dust thoroughly with the flour, shaking off any excess.

3 Heat the oil in a large non-stick frying pan over a medium heat. Add the fish and fry gently for about 10 minutes on each side.

4 Meanwhile, cut the avocados in half, remove the stones (pits) and cut in half again. Peel away the skin and cut the flesh into thin strips.

5 When the fish are cooked through and the skin is crisp and brown, transfer them to warmed serving plates. Add the avocado and corn slices. Garnish with the chopped parsley and lime slices and serve immediately.

COOK'S TIP
Using two frying pans will allow you to cook all four fish simultaneously. Alternatively, cook two and keep them hot in a covered dish in a warm oven while cooking the remaining pair.

TROUT IN WINE SAUCE WITH PLANTAIN

EXOTIC FISH FROM THE WARM CARIBBEAN WATERS, SUCH AS MAHI MAHI OR GROUPER, WOULD ADD A DISTINCTIVE FLAVOUR TO THIS TASTY DISH, WHICH IS EATEN THROUGHOUT THE REGION. IF YOU CANNOT FIND EXOTIC FISH, HOWEVER, TROUT IS IDEAL, OR YOU CAN USE ANY FILLETED WHITE FISH.

SERVES FOUR

INGREDIENTS

4 trout fillets
spice seasoning, for dusting
25g/1oz/2 tbsp butter or margarine
1–2 garlic cloves
150ml/¼ pint/⅔ cup white wine
150ml/¼ pint/⅔ cup fish stock
10ml/2 tsp clear honey
15–30ml/1–2 tbsp chopped
  fresh parsley
1 yellow plantain
salt and ground black pepper
oil, for frying
green salad, to serve

1 Season the trout fillets by coating them in the spice seasoning. Place in a shallow dish, cover with cling film (plastic wrap) and marinate in a cool place for at least 1 hour.

2 Melt the butter or margarine in a large frying pan and heat gently for 1 minute. Add the fish fillets. Sauté for about 5 minutes, until cooked through, turning carefully once. Transfer to a plate and keep hot.

3 Add the garlic, white wine, fish stock and honey to the pan and bring to the boil, stirring. Lower the heat and simmer to reduce slightly. Return the fish to the pan and spoon over the sauce. Sprinkle with the parsley and simmer gently for 2–3 minutes.

4 Meanwhile, peel the plantain, and cut it into rounds. Heat a little oil in a small frying pan and fry the plantain slices for 2–3 minutes, until golden, turning once. Transfer the fish to warmed serving plates. Stir the sauce, season and pour over the fish. Serve with the fried plantain and a green salad.

COOK'S TIP
Plantains belong to the banana family and can be green, yellow or brown, depending on how ripe they are. Unlike bananas, they must be cooked.

ESCHOVISHED FISH

THIS PICKLED FISH DISH IS OF SPANISH ORIGIN AND IS VERY POPULAR THROUGHOUT THE CARIBBEAN ISLANDS. IT GOES BY VARIOUS NAMES, INCLUDING ESCOVITCH AND CAVEACHED FISH, BUT NO MATTER WHAT THE NAME, IT INEVITABLY TASTES DELICIOUS.

SERVES SIX

INGREDIENTS
   900g/2lb cod fillet
   ½ lemon
   15ml/1 tbsp spice seasoning
   flour, for dusting
   oil, for frying
   lemon wedges, to garnish
For the sauce
   30ml/2 tbsp vegetable oil
   1 onion, sliced
   ½ red (bell) pepper, sliced
   ½ chayote (christophene), peeled,
      seeded and cut into small pieces
   2 garlic cloves, crushed
   120ml/4fl oz/½ cup malt vinegar
   75ml/5 tbsp water
   2.5ml/½ tsp ground allspice
   1 bay leaf
   1 small fresh Scotch bonnet or
      Habañero chilli, chopped
   15ml/1 tbsp soft brown sugar
   salt and ground black pepper

1 Place the fish in a shallow dish, squeeze over the lemon juice, then sprinkle with the spice seasoning. Pat the seasoning into the fish using your hands, then cover and leave to marinate in a cool place for at least 1 hour.

VARIATION
Cod fillets are very expensive so, if they are available, try using whole red snapper or red mullet, which are often used for this dish in the Caribbean.

2 Cut the cod fillet across into 7.5cm/ 3in pieces. Dust the pieces of fish with a little flour, shaking off any excess.

3 Heat the oil in a heavy frying pan and fry the fish pieces for 2–3 minutes, turning occasionally, until they are golden brown and crisp. Using a fish slice or slotted spoon, lift the cooked fish pieces out of the pan and place in a serving dish. Keep hot.

4 Make the sauce. Heat the oil in a frying pan and fry the onion for 4–5 minutes. Add the pepper, chayote and garlic and stir-fry for 2 minutes.

5 Pour in the vinegar, then add the water, allspice, bay leaf, chilli and sugar. Simmer for 5 minutes, then season. Leave to stand for 10 minutes, then pour the sauce over the fish. Serve hot, garnished with the lemon wedges.

PUMPKIN AND PRAWNS WITH DRIED SHRIMP

THIS CARIBBEAN RECIPE IS AN EXCELLENT WAY OF MAKING A SMALL AMOUNT OF SEAFOOD GO A LONG WAY. THE DRIED SHRIMPS AND COOKED PRAWNS ARE DELICIOUS WITH THE SPICED PUMPKIN.

SERVES FOUR

INGREDIENTS
  50g/2oz/⅓ cup dried shrimps
  30ml/2 tbsp vegetable oil
  25g/1oz/2 tbsp butter or margarine
  1 red onion, chopped
  800g/1¾ lb pumpkin, peeled
    and chopped
  225g/8oz peeled cooked
    prawns (shrimp)
  2.5ml/½ tsp ground cinnamon
  2.5ml/½ tsp five-spice powder
  2 garlic cloves, chopped
  2 tomatoes, chopped
  chopped fresh parsley and lime
    wedges, to garnish

1 Rinse the dried shrimps under cold water and put them in a bowl. Pour in enough hot water to cover, then leave them to soak for about 35 minutes.

2 Meanwhile, heat the oil and butter or margarine in a large frying pan. Add the onion and sauté over a medium heat for 5 minutes, until soft.

3 Add the pumpkin and cook for about 5–6 minutes, until it starts to soften. Tip in the peeled prawns and the dried shrimps with their soaking water. Stir in the cinnamon, five-spice powder and chopped garlic.

4 Add the tomatoes and cook over a gentle heat, stirring occasionally, until the pumpkin is soft.

5 Spoon on to a warmed serving plate and serve hot, garnished with the chopped parsley and lime wedges.

SALT FISH AND ACKEE

THIS IS A CLASSIC JAMAICAN DISH, THAT IS ALSO POPULAR THROUGHOUT THE CARIBBEAN. IT IS OFTEN SERVED WITH BOILED GREEN BANANAS AS WELL AS FRIED DUMPLINGS.

SERVES FOUR

INGREDIENTS

450g/1lb salt cod
25g/1oz/2 tbsp butter or margarine
30ml/2 tbsp vegetable oil
1 onion, chopped
2 garlic cloves, crushed
225g/8oz tomatoes, chopped
½ hot chilli, chopped (optional)
2.5ml/½ tsp ground black pepper
2.5ml/½ tsp dried thyme
2.5ml/½ tsp ground allspice
30ml/2 tbsp chopped spring
   onion (scallion)
540g/1lb 6oz can ackees, drained
fried dumplings, to serve

1 Place the salt cod in a bowl and pour in enough cold water to cover. Leave to soak for at least 24 hours, changing the water about five times. Drain and rinse in fresh cold water.

2 Put the salt cod in a large pan of cold water. Bring the water to the boil, then remove the fish and leave it to cool on a plate. Carefully remove and discard the skin and bones, then flake the fish and set it aside.

3 Heat the butter or margarine and oil in a large heavy frying pan over a medium heat. Add the onion and garlic and sauté for 5 minutes. Stir in the tomatoes, with the chilli, if using, and cook gently for a further 5 minutes.

4 Add the salt cod, black pepper, thyme, allspice and spring onion, stir to mix, then stir in the ackees, taking care not to crush them. If you prefer a more moist dish, add a little water or stock. Serve hot with fried dumplings.

JAMAICAN FISH CURRY

THIS RECIPE USES SOME OF THE MOST COMMON SPICES IN CARIBBEAN CUISINE, WHERE THE INFLUENCE OF INDIA IS CLEARLY VISIBLE. THE TASTE IS FOR STRONG, PUNGENT FLAVOURS RATHER THAN FIERY HEAT, AND THE RICE IS AN INTEGRAL PART OF THE DISH.

SERVES FOUR

INGREDIENTS

2 halibut steaks, total weight about
   500–675g/1¼–1½lb
30ml/2 tbsp groundnut oil
2 cardamom pods
1 cinnamon stick
6 allspice berries
4 cloves
1 large onion, chopped
3 garlic cloves, crushed
10–15ml/2–3 tsp grated fresh
   root ginger
10ml/2 tsp ground cumin
5ml/1 tsp ground coriander
2.5ml/½ tsp cayenne pepper,
   or to taste
4 tomatoes, peeled, seeded
   and chopped
1 sweet potato, about 225g/8oz,
   cut into 2cm/¾in cubes
475ml/16fl oz/2 cups fish stock
   or water
115g/4oz piece of creamed coconut
1 bay leaf
225g/8oz/generous 1 cup white
   long grain rice
salt

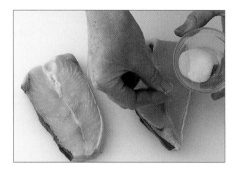

1 Rub the halibut steaks well with salt and set aside.

2 Heat the oil in a flameproof casserole dish and stir-fry the cardamom pods, cinnamon stick, allspice berries and cloves for about 3 minutes to release the delicate aromas.

3 Add the chopped onion, crushed garlic and grated ginger. Continue cooking for about 4–5 minutes over a gentle heat, stirring frequently, until the onion is soft.

4 Add the ground cumin, coriander and cayenne pepper and cook briefly, stirring all the time.

COOK'S TIP
Sweet potato discolours very quickly when cut. If you are preparing the ingredients in advance, put the cubes of potato into a bowl of cold water with 30–45ml/2–3 tbsp lemon juice until ready to use.

5 Stir in the tomatoes, sweet potato, fish stock or water, creamed coconut and bay leaf. Season well with salt. Bring to the boil, then lower the heat, cover and simmer for about 15–18 minutes, until the sweet potato is tender.

6 Cook the rice according to your preferred method.

7 Meanwhile, add the halibut steaks to the pan of curry sauce and spoon the sauce over to cover them completely. Cover the pan with a tight-fitting lid and simmer gently for about 10 minutes until the fish is just tender and flakes easily.

8 Spoon the rice into a warmed serving dish, spoon over the curry sauce and arrange the halibut steaks on top.

9 Garnish with chopped coriander (cilantro), if you like, and serve immediately.

CRAB AND CORN GUMBO

A TYPICALLY CREOLE DISH, THIS IS THICKENED WITH A CLASSIC NUT-BROWN ROUX. IT IS POPULAR ON THE CARIBBEAN ISLANDS OF MARTINIQUE AND ST BARTS.

SERVES FOUR

INGREDIENTS
  25g/1oz/2 tbsp butter or margarine
  25g/1oz/¼ cup plain
    (all-purpose) flour
  15ml/1 tbsp vegetable oil
  1 onion, finely chopped
  115g/4oz okra, trimmed and chopped
  2 garlic cloves, crushed
  15ml/1 tbsp finely chopped celery
  600ml/1 pint/2½ cups fish stock
  150ml/¼ pint/⅔ cup sherry
  15ml/1 tbsp tomato ketchup
  2.5ml/½ tsp dried oregano
  1.5ml/¼ tsp ground mixed spice
    (pumpkin pie spice)
  10ml/2 tsp Worcestershire sauce
  dash of hot pepper sauce
  2 fresh corn cobs, sliced
  450g/1lb crab claws
  fresh coriander (cilantro), to garnish

1 Melt the butter or margarine in a large heavy pan over a low heat. Add the flour and stir together to make a roux.

2 Cook for about 10 minutes, stirring constantly to prevent the mixture from burning. The roux will turn golden brown and then darken. As soon as it becomes a rich nut brown, turn the roux on to a plate, scraping it all out of the pan, and set aside.

3 Heat the oil in the same pan over a medium heat, add the chopped onion, the okra, garlic and celery and stir well. Cook for about 2–3 minutes, then add the fish stock, sherry, tomato ketchup, dried oregano, mixed spice, Worcestershire sauce and a dash of hot pepper sauce.

4 Bring to the boil, then lower the heat and simmer gently for about 10 minutes or until all the vegetables are tender. Add the roux, stirring it thoroughly into the sauce, and cook for about 3–4 minutes, until thickened.

5 Add the corn cobs and crab claws and continue to simmer gently over a low heat for about 10 minutes, until both are cooked through.

6 Spoon on to warmed serving plates and garnish with a few sprigs of fresh coriander. Serve immediately.

COOK'S TIP
The roux must not be allowed to burn. Stir it constantly over a low heat. If dark specks appear in the roux, it must be discarded and a fresh roux made.

CREOLE FISH STEW

THIS IS A SIMPLE DISH THAT LOOKS AS GOOD AS IT TASTES. IT IS A GOOD CHOICE FOR A DINNER PARTY, BUT REMEMBER TO ALLOW TIME FOR MARINATING THE FISH.

SERVES SIX

INGREDIENTS
    2 whole red bream, porgy or large
      snapper, prepared and cut into
      2.5cm/1in pieces
    30ml/2 tbsp spice seasoning
    30ml/2 tbsp malt vinegar
    flour, for dusting
    oil, for frying
For the sauce
    30ml/2 tbsp vegetable oil
    15ml/1 tbsp butter or margarine
    1 onion, finely chopped
    275g/10oz fresh tomatoes, peeled
      and finely chopped
    2 garlic cloves, crushed
    2 fresh thyme sprigs
    600ml/1 pint/2½ cups fish stock
      or water
    2.5ml/½ tsp ground cinnamon
    1 fresh hot chilli, chopped
    1 red and 1 green (bell) pepper,
      seeded and finely chopped
    salt
    fresh oregano sprigs, to garnish

1 Toss the pieces of fish with the spice seasoning and vinegar in a bowl. Cover and set aside to marinate for at least 2 hours at cool room temperature or overnight in the refrigerator.

COOK'S TIP
Take care when preparing the chilli as the capsaicin it contains is a powerful irritant and will burn the skin. Wear gloves if possible and avoid touching your face until you have removed them. Leave the chilli seeds in, or remove them for a slightly milder result.

2 When ready to cook, place a little flour in a large shallow bowl and use to coat the fish pieces, shaking off any excess flour.

3 Heat a little oil in a large frying pan. Add the fish pieces and fry for about 5 minutes, turning the pieces carefully, until golden brown, then set aside. Do not worry if the fish is not quite cooked through; it will finish cooking in the sauce.

4 To make the sauce, heat the oil and butter or margarine in a frying pan and stir-fry the onion for 5 minutes. Add the tomatoes, garlic and thyme and simmer for a further 5 minutes. Stir in the stock or water, cinnamon and chilli.

5 Add the fish pieces and the chopped peppers. Simmer until the fish is cooked and the stock has reduced to a thick sauce. Season with salt. Serve hot, garnished with the oregano.

CUBAN SEAFOOD RICE

THIS IS THE PERFECT DISH FOR A LARGE GATHERING. THE MORE PEOPLE YOU MAKE IT FOR, THE MORE TYPES OF SEAFOOD YOU CAN ADD, AND THE TASTIER IT WILL BECOME.

SERVES EIGHT

INGREDIENTS
  450g/1lb raw tiger prawns (shrimp)
  1 litre/1¾ pints/4 cups fish stock
  450g/1lb squid
  16 clams
  16 mussels
  60ml/4 tbsp olive oil
  1 onion, finely chopped
  1 fresh red chilli, seeded and
    finely chopped
  2 garlic cloves, crushed
  350g/12oz/1⅔ cups long grain rice
  45ml/3 tbsp chopped fresh
    coriander (cilantro)
  juice of 2 limes
  salt and ground black pepper

1 Peel the prawns and set them aside. Place the shells in a pan and add the fish stock. Bring to the boil, then simmer for 15 minutes. Strain into a bowl, discarding the shells.

2 Clean the squid under cold running water. Pull the tentacles away from the body. The squid's entrails will come out easily. Remove the clear piece of cartilage from inside the body cavity and discard it. Wash the body thoroughly.

3 Pull away the purplish-grey membrane that covers the body. Now cut between the tentacles and head, discarding the head and entrails. Leave the tentacles whole but discard the hard beak in the middle. Cut the body into thin rounds.

4 Scrub the clams and mussels under cold running water. Pull away the "beard" from the mussels and discard any open shells that fail to close when tapped. Place the shellfish in a bowl, cover with a wet piece of kitchen paper and put in the refrigerator until needed.

COOK'S TIP
Live shellfish are best kept in a cool moist environment. Place them in a bowl covered with wet kitchen paper and store them in the refrigerator.

5 Pour half the olive oil into a pan with a tight fitting lid. Place over a high heat. When the oil is very hot, add the squid and season well. Stir-fry for 2–3 minutes, until the squid curls and begins to brown. Remove the pieces from the pan with a slotted spoon and set aside.

6 Add the prawns to the pan and cook for 2 minutes. The moment they turn pink, remove them from the heat.

7 Pour the remaining oil into the pan. Stir in the onion and sauté over a low heat for 5 minutes. Add the chilli and garlic and cook for 2 minutes. Tip in the rice, and cook, stirring, for 1 minute, until lightly toasted but not coloured.

8 Add the prawn stock and bring to the boil. Cover, lower the heat and simmer, for 15–18 minutes.

9 Add the clams and mussels and cover the pan. Cook for 3–4 minutes, until their shells open. Remove from the heat and discard any that have remained closed. Stir the cooked squid, prawns, coriander and lime juice into the rice. Season and serve immediately.

KING PRAWNS IN SWEETCORN SAUCE

MAKE THIS DELICIOUS SAUCE TO USE AS A FILLING FOR BAKED SWEET POTATOES. SERVE WITH A SIDE SALAD FOR A HEARTY AND NUTRITIOUS LUNCH.

SERVES FOUR

INGREDIENTS
    24–30 large raw prawns (shrimp)
    spice seasoning, for dusting
    juice of 1 lemon
    30ml/2 tbsp butter or margarine
    1 onion, chopped
    2 garlic cloves, crushed
    30ml/2 tbsp tomato purée (paste)
    2.5ml/½ tsp dried thyme
    2.5ml/½ tsp ground cinnamon
    15ml/1 tbsp chopped fresh coriander
        (cilantro)
    ½ hot chilli pepper, chopped
    175g/6oz frozen or canned corn
    300ml/½ pint/1¼ cups coconut milk
    chopped fresh coriander, to garnish

1 Sprinkle the prawns with spice seasoning and lemon juice and marinate in a cool place for an hour.

2 Melt the butter or margarine in a pan and fry the onion and garlic for 5 minutes, until slightly softened. Add the prawns and cook for a few minutes, stirring occasionally until cooked through and pink.

3 Transfer the prawns, onion and garlic to a bowl, leaving behind some of the buttery liquid. Add the tomato pureé and cook over a low heat, stirring.

4 Add the thyme, cinnamon, coriander and hot pepper to the pan and stir well.

5 Blend the corn (reserving 15ml/ 1 tbsp) in a blender or food processor with the coconut milk. Add to the pan and simmer until reduced.

6 Add the prawns and reserved corn, and simmer for 5 minutes. Serve hot, garnished with coriander.

PRAWNS AND SALT FISH WITH OKRA

THIS UNUSUAL MIXTURE OF SALTFISH AND PRAWNS IS ENHANCED BY THE ADDITION OF OKRA. ANY TYPE OF SALTFISH MAY BE USED, BUT COD HAS THE BEST FLAVOUR.

SERVES FOUR

INGREDIENTS
    450g/1lb raw prawns (shrimp),
        peeled
    15ml/1 tbsp spice seasoning
    25g/1oz/2 tbsp butter or margarine
    15ml/1 tbsp olive oil
    2 shallots, finely chopped
    1 garlic clove, crushed
    350g/12oz okra, topped, tailed and
        cut into 2.5cm/1in lengths
    5ml/1 tsp curry powder
    10ml/2 tsp shrimp paste
    15ml/1 tbsp chopped fresh coriander
        (cilantro)
    15ml/1 tbsp lemon juice
    175g/6oz prepared salt fish

1 Season the prawns with the spice seasoning and leave to marinate in a cool place for about 1 hour.

2 Heat the butter or margarine and olive oil in a large frying pan or wok over a moderate heat and stir-fry the shallots and garlic for 5 minutes. Add the okra, curry powder and shrimp paste, stir well and cook for 10 minutes, or until tender.

3 Add 30ml/2 tbsp water, coriander, lemon juice, prawns and salt fish, and cook gently for 5–10 minutes. Adjust the seasoning and serve hot.

COOK'S TIP
Soak the salt fish for 12 hours, changing the water two or three times. Rinse, bring to the boil in fresh water, then leave to cool.

MEAT AND POULTRY

Whether roasted or made into stews and curries, meat — beef, pork and lamb — is cooked with plenty of herbs and spices, and dishes usually include the addition of local vegetables or beans. Chicken is the meat most frequently eaten in the Caribbean — the Sunday roast is very popular. For weekday meals portions of chicken and turkey are typically cooked in rich sauces.

PEPPERED STEAK IN SHERRY CREAM SAUCE

THE VAST SUBCONTINENT OF SOUTH AMERICA IS SUBJECT TO MANY CULINARY INFLUENCES, ALL OF WHICH HARMONIZE WITH THE NATIVE RECIPES OF EACH COUNTRY. VERSIONS OF THIS DISH ARE TO BE FOUND ALL OVER THE WORLD, BUT THE ADDITION OF PLANTAIN IS A CARIBBEAN ADAPTATION.

2 Season the meat with pepper and spice seasoning, place in a shallow dish and cover. Leave to marinate in a cool place for 30 minutes.

3 Melt the butter in a large frying pan and sauté the strips of steak for about 4–5 minutes, until browned on all sides. Using a slotted spoon, transfer to a warm plate and set aside.

4 Add the shallots and garlic, fry gently for 2–3 minutes, then stir in the sherry and water. Simmer for 5 minutes.

SERVES FOUR

INGREDIENTS
    675g/1½lb frying steak
    5ml/1 tsp spice seasoning
    25g/1oz/2 tbsp butter
    6–8 shallots, sliced
    2 garlic cloves, crushed
    120ml/4fl oz/½ cup sherry
    45ml/3 tbsp water
    75ml/5 tbsp single (light) cream
    salt and ground black pepper
    chopped fresh chives, to garnish
    cooked plantain, to serve

1 Cut the frying steak into thin strips, of even length and thickness, discarding any fat or gristle.

5 Stir in the cream and season. Return the meat to the pan and heat through. Serve with plantain and chopped chives.

OXTAIL AND BUTTER BEANS

THIS IS A TRADITIONAL CARIBBEAN STEW — OLD-FASHIONED, ECONOMICAL AND FULL OF GOODNESS. IT REQUIRES PATIENCE BECAUSE OF THE LONG COOKING TIME. THERE IS NOT MUCH MEAT ON THE OXTAIL, SO IT IS NECESSARY TO BUY A LARGE AMOUNT.

SERVES FOUR

INGREDIENTS

1.6kg/3½lb oxtail, chopped into pieces
1 onion, finely chopped
3 bay leaves
4 fresh thyme sprigs
3 whole cloves
1.75 litres/3 pints/7½ cups water
175g/6oz/scant 1 cup dried
   butter (lima) beans, soaked overnight
2 garlic cloves, crushed
15ml/1 tbsp tomato purée (paste)
400g/14oz can chopped tomatoes
5ml/1 tsp ground allspice
1 fresh hot chilli
salt and ground black pepper

1 Put the pieces of oxtail in a large heavy pan, add the chopped onion, bay leaves, thyme and cloves and cover with water. Bring to the boil.

2 Reduce the heat, cover the pan and simmer gently for at least 2½ hours or until the meat is very tender. If the meat looks like it might dry out, add a little extra water, being careful not to add too much at one time.

3 Meanwhile, drain the butter beans and tip them into a large pan. Pour in water to cover. Bring to the boil, lower the heat and simmer for about 1–1¼ hours or until just tender. Drain and set aside until ready to use.

COOK'S TIP
Unless you are confident using a meat cleaver to chop the oxtail into short lengths, ask your butcher to do it for you.

VARIATION
Haricot (navy) beans can be used in the same way as butter beans in the recipe.

4 When the oxtail is cooked, add the garlic, tomato purée, tomatoes, allspice, and chilli, and season. Add the beans, simmer for 20 minutes, then serve.

PORK ROASTED WITH HERBS, SPICES AND RUM

IN THE CARIBBEAN, THIS SPICY ROAST PORK IS A FAVOURITE DISH THAT IS USUALLY COOKED ON A BARBECUE AND SERVED ON SPECIAL OCCASIONS AS PART OF A BUFFET.

SERVES EIGHT

INGREDIENTS
    2 garlic cloves, crushed
    45ml/3 tbsp soy sauce
    15ml/1 tbsp malt vinegar
    15ml/1 tbsp finely chopped celery
    30ml/2 tbsp chopped spring
      onion (scallion)
    7.5ml/1½ tsp dried thyme
    5ml/1 tsp dried sage
    2.5ml/½ tsp ground mixed spice
      (pumpkin pie spice)
    10ml/2 tsp curry powder
    120ml/4fl oz/½ cup rum
    15ml/1 tbsp demerara (raw) sugar
    1.6kg/3½lb boned loin of pork
    salt and ground black pepper
    spring onion (scallion) curls,
      to garnish
    creamed sweet potato, to serve
For the sauce
    25g/1oz/2 tbsp butter or
      margarine, diced
    15ml/1 tbsp tomato purée (paste)
    300ml/½ pint/1¼ cups chicken or
      pork stock
    15ml/1 tbsp chopped fresh parsley
    15ml/1 tbsp demerara (raw) sugar
    hot pepper sauce, to taste

1 In a bowl, mix the garlic, soy sauce, vinegar, celery, spring onion, thyme, sage, spice, curry powder, rum, and sugar. Add a little salt and pepper.

2 Open out the pork and slash the meat, without cutting through it completely. Place it in a shallow dish. Spread most of the spice mixture all over the pork, pressing it well into the slashes. Rub the outside of the joint with the remaining mixture, cover the dish with clear film (plastic wrap) and chill in the refrigerator overnight.

COOK'S TIP
In the Caribbean, pork is baked until it is very well done, so reduce the cooking time if you prefer meat slightly more moist. To get the full flavour from the marinade, start preparation the day before.

3 Preheat the oven to 190°C/375°F/ Gas 5. Roll the meat up, then tie it tightly in several places with strong cotton string to hold the meat together.

4 Spread a large piece of foil across a roasting pan and place the marinated pork loin in the centre. Baste the pork with a few spoonfuls of the marinade and wrap the foil around the meat.

5 Roast the pork in the oven for 1¾ hours, then slide the foil out from under the meat and discard it. Baste the pork with any remaining marinade and cook for a further 1 hour. Check occasionally that the meat is not drying out and baste with the pan juices.

6 Meanwhile, make the sauce. Transfer the pork to a warmed serving dish, cover with foil and leave to stand in a warm place for 15 minutes. Pour the pan juices into a pan. Add the butter or margarine, tomato purée, stock, parsley and sugar, with hot pepper sauce and salt to taste. Simmer until reduced.

7 Serve the pork sliced, with the creamed sweet potato. Garnish with the spring onion curls and serve the sauce separately.

CARIBBEAN LAMB CURRY

THIS JAMAICAN DISH IS POPULARLY KNOWN AS CURRIED GOAT OR CURRY GOAT, ALTHOUGH KID, LAMB OR MUTTON ARE EQUALLY LIKELY TO BE USED TO MAKE IT.

SERVES SIX

INGREDIENTS

   900g/2lb boned leg of mutton
     or lamb
   50g/2oz/4 tbsp curry powder
   3 garlic cloves, crushed
   1 large onion, chopped
   leaves from 4 fresh thyme sprigs,
     or 5ml/1 tsp dried thyme
   3 bay leaves
   5ml/1 tsp ground allspice
   30ml/2 tbsp vegetable oil
   50g/2oz/¼ cup butter or margarine
   900ml/1½ pints/3¾ cups lamb stock
     or water
   1 fresh hot chilli, chopped
   fresh coriander (cilantro) sprigs,
     to garnish
   cooked rice, to serve

3 Melt the butter or margarine in a large heavy pan. Add the seasoned mutton or lamb and fry over a medium heat for about 10 minutes, turning the meat frequently.

4 Stir in the stock or water and chilli, and bring to the boil. Lower the heat, cover and simmer for 1½ hours or until the meat is tender. Garnish with coriander and serve with rice.

1 Cut the meat into 5cm/2in cubes, discarding excess fat and any gristle. Place it in a large bowl.

2 Add the curry powder, garlic, onion, thyme, bay leaves, allspice and oil. Mix well, then cover the bowl and place in the refrigerator. Marinate for at least 3 hours or overnight.

"SEASONED-UP" LAMB IN SPINACH SAUCE

IN THE CARIBBEAN, ESPECIALLY ON THE ENGLISH-SPEAKING ISLANDS, YOU WILL OFTEN HEAR DISHES DESCRIBED AS "SEASONED UP". THIS REFERS TO THE USE OF A SPICY RUB OR MARINADE, A TECHNIQUE THAT WORKS WELL WITH CHEAPER CUTS OF MEAT.

SERVES FOUR

INGREDIENTS

675g/1½lb boneless lamb, cubed
2.5ml/½ tsp ground ginger
2.5ml/½ tsp dried thyme
30ml/2 tbsp olive oil
1 onion, chopped
2 garlic cloves, crushed
15ml/1 tbsp tomato purée (paste)
½ fresh hot chilli, chopped (optional)
600ml/1 pint/2½ cups lamb stock
  or water
115g/4oz fresh spinach, finely
  chopped
salt and ground black pepper

1 Put the lamb cubes in a dish. Sprinkle over the ginger and thyme, season and mix well to coat. Cover and marinate for at least 2 hours or overnight in the refrigerator.

2 Heat the olive oil in a heavy pan, add the onion and garlic and fry gently for 5 minutes or until the onion is soft.

3 Add the lamb with the tomato purée and chilli, if using. Fry over a medium heat for about 5 minutes, stirring frequently, then add the lamb stock or water. Cover and simmer for about 30 minutes, until the lamb is tender.

4 Stir in the spinach and simmer for around 8 minutes. Serve hot.

LAMB PELAU

INDIAN IMMIGRANTS INTRODUCED THE PILAU TO THE CARIBBEAN. THE NAME HAS CHANGED SLIGHTLY, BUT RICE DISHES LIKE THIS ONE REMAIN TRUE TO THEIR ORIGINS.

SERVES FOUR

INGREDIENTS

450g/1lb stewing lamb
15ml/1 tbsp curry powder
1 onion, finely chopped
2 garlic cloves, crushed
2.5ml/½ tsp dried thyme
2.5ml/½ tsp dried oregano
1 fresh or dried chilli
25g/1oz/2 tbsp butter or margarine,
  plus extra for serving
600ml/1 pint/2½ cups beef
  stock, chicken stock or
  coconut milk
5ml/1 tsp ground black pepper
2 tomatoes, chopped
10ml/2 tsp sugar
30ml/2 tbsp chopped spring
  onion (scallion)
450g/1lb/2½ cups basmati rice
spring onion strips, to garnish

1 Cut the lamb into cubes and place in a dish. Add the curry powder, onion, garlic, herbs and chilli and stir well. Cover with clear film (plastic wrap) and leave to marinate for 1 hour.

2 Melt the butter or margarine in a pan and fry the lamb for 5–10 minutes. Pour in the stock or coconut milk, bring to the boil, then lower the heat and simmer for 35 minutes or until tender.

3 Add the black pepper, tomatoes, sugar, chopped spring onion and rice. Stir well and reduce the heat. Make sure that the rice is covered by 2.5cm/1in of liquid; add a little water if necessary. Cover the pan; simmer the pelau for 25 minutes or until the rice has absorbed the liquid and is cooked. Spoon into a serving bowl and stir in a little extra butter or margarine. Garnish with spring onion strips and serve.

BARBECUED JERK CHICKEN

JERK SEASONING IS A BLEND OF HERBS AND SPICES THAT IS RUBBED INTO MEAT BEFORE IT IS COOKED OVER CHARCOAL SPRINKLED WITH PIMIENTO BERRIES. IN JAMAICA, JERK SEASONING WAS ORIGINALLY USED ONLY FOR PORK, BUT JERKED CHICKEN TASTES JUST AS GOOD.

2 Make several lengthways slits in the flesh on the chicken pieces. Place the chicken pieces in a dish and spoon the jerk seasoning over them. Use your hands to rub the seasoning into the chicken, especially into the slits.

3 Cover with clear film (plastic wrap) and marinate for at least 4–6 hours or overnight in the refrigerator.

SERVES FOUR

INGREDIENTS
   8 chicken pieces
   oil, for brushing
   salad leaves, to serve
For the jerk seasoning
   5ml/1 tsp ground allspice
   5ml/1 tsp ground cinnamon
   5ml/1 tsp dried thyme
   1.5ml/¼ tsp freshly grated nutmeg
   10ml/2 tsp demerara (raw) sugar
   2 garlic cloves, crushed
   15ml/1 tbsp finely chopped onion
   15ml/1 tbsp chopped spring
     onion (scallion)
   15ml/1 tbsp vinegar
   30ml/2 tbsp oil
   15ml/1 tbsp lime juice
   1 fresh hot chilli pepper, chopped
   salt and ground black pepper

1 Make the jerk seasoning. Combine the ground allspice, cinnamon, thyme, grated nutmeg, sugar, garlic, both types of onion, vinegar, oil, lime juice and chilli pepper in a small bowl. Use a fork to mash them together until a thick paste is formed. Season to taste with a little salt and plenty of ground black pepper.

4 Preheat the grill (broiler) or prepare the barbecue. Shake off any excess seasoning from the chicken and brush the pieces with oil. Either place on a baking sheet and grill (broil) for 45 minutes, or cook on the barbecue for about 30 minutes. Whichever method you choose, it is important to turn the chicken pieces frequently. Serve hot with salad leaves.

COOK'S TIP
The flavour is best if you marinate the chicken overnight. If cooking on the barbecue, sprinkle the charcoal with aromatic herbs, such as rosemary or bay leaves, for even more flavour.

THYME AND LIME CHICKEN

LIMES GROWN IN THE CARIBBEAN TEND TO BE PALER THAN THE ONES IN OUR SUPERMARKETS, BUT THEY ARE JUICY AND FULL OF FLAVOUR. THIS RECIPE, WHICH COMBINES THEM WITH FRAGRANT THYME, IS A GREAT VEHICLE FOR THEM.

SERVES FOUR

INGREDIENTS
    8 chicken thighs
    30ml/2 tbsp chopped spring
      onion (scallion)
    10ml/2 tsp chopped fresh thyme or
      5ml/1 tsp dried thyme
    2 garlic cloves, crushed
    juice of 2 limes or 1 lemon
    75g/3oz/6 tbsp butter, melted
    salt and ground black pepper
    cooked rice, to serve
To garnish
    lime slices
    fresh coriander (cilantro) sprigs

3 Spoon the remaining butter evenly over the top of the chicken pieces. Cover the dish tightly with clear film (plastic wrap) and leave to marinate for at least 3–4 hours in the refrigerator. For the best flavour, prepare the chicken the day before and leave to marinate overnight.

4 Preheat the oven to 190°C/375°F/Gas 5. Remove the film and cover the chicken with foil. Bake for about 1 hour, then remove the foil and cook for a further 5–10 minutes, until the chicken turns golden brown. Garnish with lime slices and fresh coriander and serve with rice.

1 Put the chicken thighs skin side down in a baking dish or roasting pan. Using a sharp knife, make a lengthways slit along the thigh bone of each. Mix the spring onion with a little salt and pepper and press the mixture into the slits.

2 Mix the thyme, garlic and lime or lemon juice in a small bowl. Add 50g/2oz/4 tbsp of the butter and mix well, then spoon a little of the mixture over each chicken thigh, spreading evenly.

SPICY FRIED CHICKEN

This traditional Caribbean crispy chicken dish is superb eaten hot or cold. Served with a salad or vegetables, it makes a delicious lunch and is also perfect for picnics or snacks.

SERVES FOUR

INGREDIENTS

4 chicken drumsticks
4 chicken thighs
10ml/2 tsp curry powder
2.5ml/½ tsp garlic granules or
  1 garlic clove, crushed
2.5ml/½ tsp ground black pepper
2.5ml/½ tsp paprika
about 300ml/½ pint/1¼ cups milk
oil, for deep frying
50g/2oz/½ cup plain
  (all-purpose) flour
salt
dressed salad leaves, to serve

1 Sprinkle the chicken pieces with curry powder, garlic, pepper, paprika and a little salt. Rub into the chicken, then cover and marinate for at least 2 hours, or overnight in the refrigerator.

2 Preheat the oven to 180ºC/350ºF/ Gas 4. Cover the chicken with milk and leave to stand for a further 15 minutes.

3 Heat the oil in a large pan or deep-fryer and tip the flour on to a plate. Dip the chicken pieces in flour and add to the oil, taking care not to overcrowd the pan. Fry until golden, but not fully cooked.

4 Remove the chicken pieces with a slotted spoon and place on a baking sheet. Continue until all the chicken pieces have been fried.

5 Place the baking sheet in the oven and bake the chicken for around 30 minutes. Serve hot or cold with dressed salad leaves.

SUNDAY ROAST CHICKEN

MUCH OF THE PREPARATION FOR THIS DISH IS DONE THE NIGHT BEFORE, MAKING IT IDEAL FOR A FAMILY LUNCH. THE CHICKEN IS SUCCULENT AND FULL OF FLAVOUR, WITH A RICH GRAVY.

SERVES SIX

INGREDIENTS

1.6kg/3½lb chicken
5ml/1 tsp paprika
5ml/1 tsp dried thyme
2.5ml/½ tsp dried tarragon
5ml/1 tsp garlic granules or 1 garlic
  clove, crushed
15ml/1 tbsp lemon juice
30ml/2 tbsp clear honey
45ml/3 tbsp dark rum
melted butter, for basting
300ml/½ pint/1¼ cups chicken stock
lime quarters, to garnish

1 Place the chicken in a roasting pan and sprinkle with paprika, thyme, tarragon, garlic and salt and pepper. Rub the mixture all over the chicken, including underneath the skin. Cover with clear film (plastic wrap) and leave to marinate for at least 2 hours or overnight in the refrigerator.

2 Preheat the oven to 190°C/375°F/ Gas 5. Mix the lemon, honey and rum in a bowl. Stir well, then pour over and under the chicken skin, rubbing it in well to ensure the flavours are absorbed.

3 Spoon melted butter all over the chicken, then transfer to the oven and roast for 1½–2 hours, until fully cooked.

VARIATION
Extra herbs and rum can be used to make a richer, tastier gravy, if you like.

4 Transfer the chicken to a serving dish while you make the gravy. Pour the pan juices into a small pan. Add the chicken stock. Simmer for 10 minutes or until the gravy has reduced and thickened slightly. Adjust the seasoning and pour into a serving jug (pitcher). Garnish the chicken with the lime and serve.

PEANUT CHICKEN

THE RICH SAUCE FOR THIS POPULAR CARIBBEAN DISH IS BEST MADE WITH SMOOTH PEANUT BUTTER, ALTHOUGH IT CAN ALSO BE MADE WITH GROUND PEANUTS.

SERVES FOUR

INGREDIENTS
    900g/2lb boneless chicken
      breast portions, skinned and
      cut into cubes
    2 garlic cloves, crushed
    2.5ml/½ tsp dried thyme
    2.5ml/½ tsp ground black pepper
    15ml/1 tbsp curry powder
    15ml/1 tbsp lemon juice
    25g/1oz/2 tbsp butter or margarine
    1 onion, chopped
    45ml/3 tbsp chopped tomatoes
    1 fresh hot chilli, seeded
      and chopped
    30ml/2 tbsp smooth peanut butter
    450ml/¾ pint/scant 2 cups
      warm water
    salt
    fresh coriander (cilantro) sprigs,
      to garnish
    fried plantain, to serve
    okra, to serve

1 Put the chicken in a large bowl and stir in the garlic, thyme, black pepper, curry powder, lemon juice and a little salt. Cover and marinate in a cool place for 3–4 hours.

2 Melt the butter or margarine in a large pan. Add the onion, sauté gently for 5 minutes, then add the seasoned chicken. Fry over a medium heat for 10 minutes, turning frequently, and then stir in the tomatoes and chilli.

3 In a small bowl, blend the peanut butter to a smooth paste with a little of the warm water and stir this paste into the chicken mixture.

4 Gradually stir in the remaining water, then simmer gently for about 30 minutes or until the chicken is fully cooked. Add a little more water if the sauce begins to dry out. Garnish with sprigs of fresh coriander and serve hot with slices of fried plantain and okra.

BREAST OF TURKEY WITH MANGO AND WINE

FRESH TROPICAL MANGO AND WARM CINNAMON COMBINE TO GIVE A REAL TASTE OF THE CARIBBEAN.

SERVES FOUR

INGREDIENTS
    4 turkey breast fillets
    1 small ripe mango
    1 garlic clove, crushed
    1.5ml/¼ tsp ground cinnamon
    15ml/1 tbsp finely chopped
      fresh parsley
    15ml/1 tbsp crushed cream crackers
      (oyster crackers)
    40g/1½oz/3 tbsp butter or margarine
    1 garlic clove, crushed
    6 shallots, sliced
    150ml/¼ pint/⅔ cup white wine
    salt and ground black pepper
    diced fresh mango and chopped fresh
      parsley, to garnish

1 Cut a slit horizontally into each turkey fillet to make a pocket. Using a sharp knife, peel the mango and cut the flesh off the stone (pit). Finely chop enough of the flesh to make 30ml/2 tbsp and roughly dice the remainder.

2 Mix the garlic, cinnamon, parsley, cracker crumbs and finely chopped mango in a bowl. Add 15ml/1 tbsp of the butter or margarine with salt and pepper to taste and mash together.

3 Spoon a little of the mango mixture into each of the pockets in the turkey breast fillets and close, securing with a wooden cocktail stick (toothpick) if necessary. Season with a little extra ground black pepper.

4 Melt the remaining butter in a frying pan and sauté the crushed garlic and sliced shallots for about 5 minutes. Add the turkey fillets and cook for 15 minutes, turning once. Add the wine, cover and simmer for 5–10 minutes, until the turkey is cooked. Add the mango, heat, and serve garnished with parsley.

VEGETARIAN DISHES AND SALADS

Vegetarianism is not widespread in the Caribbean, but beans, corn and what might be considered exotic vegetables and fruits, such as sweet potatoes, plantain and aubergines, are used extensively. The recipes in this section make appetizing meals that can be enjoyed by everyone — not just vegetarians — either as a light lunch, or as part of a main meal.

MACARONI CHEESE PIE

MACARONI CHEESE IS A FAVOURITE DISH ON THE ISLAND OF BARBADOS, WHERE IT IS OFTEN SERVED AS AN ACCOMPANIMENT, INSTEAD OF A STARCHY VEGETABLE SUCH AS POTATO. THIS TREATMENT MAKES AN EXCELLENT VEGETARIAN MAIN COURSE.

3 Stir in the mustard and cinnamon, with two-thirds of the cheese. Season to taste. Cook gently, stirring frequently, until the cheese has melted, then remove from the heat and whisk in the egg. Cover closely and set aside.

4 Heat the remaining butter or margarine in a small frying pan and cook the spring onion, chopped tomatoes and corn over a gentle heat for 5–10 minutes.

5 Tip half the cooked macaroni into a greased ovenproof dish. Pour over half the cheese sauce and mix well, then spoon the tomato and corn mixture evenly over the mixture.

6 Tip the remaining macaroni into the pan containing the cheese sauce, stir well and then spread carefully over the tomato and corn mixture.

SERVES FOUR

INGREDIENTS
225g/8oz/2 cups macaroni
40g/1½oz/3 tbsp butter or margarine
20g/¾oz/3 tbsp plain
  (all-purpose) flour
450ml/¾ pint/scant 2 cups milk
5ml/1 tsp mild mustard
2.5ml/½ tsp ground cinnamon
175g/6oz mature (sharp) Cheddar
  cheese, grated
1 egg, beaten
15ml/1 tbsp butter or margarine
25g/1oz/2 tbsp chopped spring
  onion (scallion)
40g/1½oz/3 tbsp canned
  chopped tomatoes
115g/4oz/⅔ cup corn kernels
salt and ground black pepper
chopped fresh parsley, to garnish

1 Heat the oven to 180°C/350°F/Gas 4. Cook the macaroni in a pan of salted boiling water for 10 minutes. Drain, rinse under cold water and drain again.

2 Melt 25g/1oz/2 tbsp of the butter in a pan and add the flour. Cook for 1 minute, then add the milk, whisking constantly. Heat until the mixture boils, then simmer gently for 5–10 minutes.

7 Top with the remaining grated cheese. Bake for about 45 minutes, or until the top is golden and bubbly. If possible, leave to stand for 30 minutes before serving, garnished with parsley.

RED BEAN CHILLI

SATISFYING, SPICY AND SIMPLE TO PREPARE, THIS VEGETARIAN CARIBBEAN VERSION OF THE CLASSIC MEXICAN CHILLI IS COMFORT FOOD AT ITS BEST. EXPERIMENT WITH DIFFERENT TYPES OF CHILLI PEPPERS, INCLUDING DRIED VARIETIES LIKE THE MEXICAN CHIPOTLES.

SERVES FOUR

INGREDIENTS
  30ml/2 tbsp vegetable oil
  1 onion, chopped
  400g/14oz can chopped tomatoes
  2 garlic cloves, crushed
  300ml/½ pint/1¼ cups white wine
  about 300ml/½ pint/1¼ cups
    vegetable stock
  115g/4oz/1 cup red lentils
  2 fresh thyme sprigs or 5ml/1 tsp
    dried thyme
  10ml/2 tsp ground cumin
  45ml/3 tbsp dark soy sauce
  ½ fresh hot chilli, seeded and
    finely chopped
  5ml/1 tsp ground mixed spice
    (pumpkin pie spice)
  15ml/1 tbsp oyster sauce (optional)
  225g/8oz can red kidney
    beans, drained
  10ml/2 tsp sugar
  salt
  boiled white rice with corn,
    to serve

1 Heat the oil in a pan and fry the onion for 2–3 minutes, until slightly softened.

2 Add the tomatoes and garlic, cook for about 10 minutes, then stir in the white wine and vegetable stock.

VARIATION
This vegetarian chilli can be adapted to accommodate meat-eaters by substituting either minced (ground) beef or lamb for the lentils.

3 Stir in the lentils, thyme, cumin, soy sauce, chilli, spice and oyster sauce, if using.

COOK'S TIP
Fiery chillies can irritate the skin, so always wash your hands thoroughly after handling them and avoid touching your eyes.

4 Cover and simmer for 40 minutes or until the lentils are cooked, stirring occasionally and adding more water if the lentils begin to dry out.

5 Stir in the kidney beans and sugar and cook for 10 minutes more. Season to taste and serve with boiled white rice and corn.

SPICY VEGETABLE CHOW MEIN

CHOW MEIN IS POPULAR IN GUYANA, WHERE IT IS USUALLY MADE WITH SHREDDED CHICKEN OR PRAWNS. THIS VEGETARIAN VERSION CAN BE ADAPTED TO SUIT ALL TASTES.

SERVES THREE

INGREDIENTS

225g/8oz egg noodles
115g/4oz/¾ cup fine green beans
30–45ml/2–3 tbsp vegetable oil
2 garlic cloves, crushed
1 onion, chopped
1 small red (bell) pepper, chopped
1 small green (bell) pepper, chopped
2 celery sticks, finely chopped
2.5ml/½ tsp five-spice powder
1 vegetable stock (bouillon) cube
2.5ml/½ tsp ground black pepper
15ml/1 tbsp soy sauce (optional)
salt

COOK'S TIP
Shredded omelette or sliced hard-boiled eggs are popular garnishes for chow mein.

1 Cook the noodles in a large pan of salted boiling water for 10 minutes or according to the instructions on the packet. Drain and cool. Blanch the beans.

2 Heat the oil in a wok or large frying pan and stir-fry the garlic, onion, red and green pepper, beans and celery, tossing them together to mix.

3 Add the five-spice powder, vegetable stock cube and ground black pepper, stir well and cook for 5 minutes until the vegetables are just tender but still slightly crunchy.

4 Stir in the noodles and soy sauce, if using. Taste the chow mein and season with salt if required. Serve immediately.

AUBERGINES STUFFED WITH SWEET POTATO

SLICES OF AUBERGINE ROLLED AROUND A SWEET POTATO AND CHEESE FILLING MAKE AN UNUSUAL CARIBBEAN SUPPER DISH, OR TRY THEM AS AN APPETIZER FOR A VEGETARIAN MEAL.

SERVES FOUR

INGREDIENTS

225g/8oz/I cup sweet potatoes,
   peeled and quartered
2.5ml/½ tsp chopped fresh thyme
75g/3oz/¾ cup Cheddar
   cheese, diced
25g/1oz/2 tbsp chopped spring
   onion (scallion)
15ml/1 tbsp each chopped red and
   green (bell) pepper
1 garlic clove, crushed
2 large aubergines (eggplants)
30ml/2 tbsp plain
   (all-purpose) flour
15ml/1 tbsp spice seasoning
olive oil, for frying
butter, for greasing
2 tomatoes, sliced
salt and ground black pepper
chopped fresh parsley,
   to garnish

1 Preheat the oven to 180°C/350°F/ Gas 4. Cook the sweet potatoes in a pan of boiling water for 15–20 minutes, until tender, then drain and mash.

2 Add the thyme, cheese, spring onion, peppers and garlic. Mix well and season.

3 Cut each aubergine lengthways into four slices. Mix the flour and spice seasoning on a plate and dust over each aubergine slice.

4 Heat a little oil in a large frying pan and fry each aubergine slice until browned, but not fully cooked. Drain and cool. Spoon a little of the potato mixture into the middle of each aubergine slice and roll up.

5 Butter two large pieces of foil and cover with the slices of tomato. Place four rolls on each piece of foil. Wrap up the parcels and bake for 20 minutes. Serve hot, garnished with the parsley.

SPINACH PLANTAIN ROUNDS

THIS DELECTABLE WAY OF SERVING PLANTAINS IS POPULAR THROUGHOUT THE CARIBBEAN ISLANDS. THE PLANTAINS MUST BE FAIRLY RIPE, BUT STILL FIRM. THE ROUNDS CAN BE SERVED EITHER HOT OR COLD, WITH A SALAD, OR AS A VEGETABLE ACCOMPANIMENT.

SERVES FOUR

INGREDIENTS

2 large ripe plantains
oil, for frying
15g/½oz/2 tbsp butter or margarine
25g/1oz/2 tbsp finely chopped onion
2 garlic cloves, crushed
450g/1lb fresh spinach, chopped
pinch of freshly grated nutmeg
1 egg, beaten
wholemeal (whole-wheat) flour,
  for dusting
salt and ground black pepper

1 Using a small sharp knife, carefully cut each plantain lengthways into four pieces.

2 Heat a little oil in a large frying pan and fry the pieces of plantain on both sides until golden brown but not fully cooked. Lift out and drain on kitchen paper. Reserve the oil in the pan.

3 Melt the butter or margarine in a separate pan and sauté the onion and garlic for 2–3 minutes, until the onion is soft. Add the spinach and nutmeg, with salt and pepper to taste. Cover and cook for about 5 minutes, until the spinach has wilted. Cool, then tip into a sieve (strainer) and press out any excess moisture.

4 Curl the plantain pieces into rings and secure each ring with half a wooden cocktail stick (toothpick). Pack each ring with a little of the spinach mixture.

5 Place the egg and flour in two separate shallow dishes. Add a little more oil to the frying pan, if necessary, and heat until medium hot. Dip the plantain rings in the egg and then in the flour and fry on both sides for 1–2 minutes until golden brown. Drain on kitchen paper and serve.

PEPPERY BEAN SALAD

THIS PRETTY CARIBBEAN SALAD USES CANNED BEANS FOR SPEED AND CONVENIENCE. THE CONTRAST BETWEEN THE CRISP RADISHES AND PEPPERS AND THE SOFTER TEXTURE OF THE BEANS IS ONE REASON WHY IT WORKS SO WELL. THE TASTY DRESSING PLAYS A PART, TOO.

SERVES SIX

INGREDIENTS
  425g/15oz can kidney beans, drained
  425g/15oz can black-eyed beans
    (peas), drained
  425g/15oz can chickpeas, drained
  ¼ red (bell) pepper
  ¼ green (bell) pepper
  6 radishes
  15ml/1 tbsp chopped spring
    onion (scallion)
  sliced spring onion, to garnish
For the dressing
  5ml/1 tsp ground cumin
  15ml/1 tbsp tomato ketchup
  30ml/2 tbsp olive oil
  15ml/1 tbsp white wine vinegar
  1 garlic clove, crushed
  2.5ml/½ tsp hot pepper sauce
  salt

1 Drain the canned beans and chickpeas into a colander and rinse them thoroughly under cold running water. Shake off the excess water and tip them into a large salad bowl.

2 Core, seed and roughly chop the peppers. Trim the radishes and slice them thinly. Add to the beans with the chopped pepper and spring onion.

COOK'S TIP
For maximum flavour, it is best to allow the ingredients to marinate for at least 3–4 hours.

3 In a small bowl, mix the ground cumin, ketchup, olive oil, white wine vinegar and garlic. Add the hot pepper sauce and a little salt to taste and stir again until thoroughly mixed.

4 Pour the dressing over the salad and mix thoroughly with a fork. Cover with clear film (plastic wrap) and chill for at least 1 hour before serving, garnished with sliced spring onion.

SPICY POTATO SALAD

ADDING JUST A LITTLE CHILLI GIVES THIS CARIBBEAN SALAD A DELECTABLE SPICY FLAVOUR, WHICH IS BALANCED BY THE CREAMY DRESSING. IT MAKES A GOOD ACCOMPANIMENT TO GRILLED MEAT OR FISH.

SERVES SIX

INGREDIENTS
  900g/2lb new potatoes, peeled
  2 red (bell) peppers
  2 celery sticks
  1 shallot
  2–3 spring onions (scallions)
  1 fresh green chilli
  1 garlic clove, crushed
  10ml/2 tsp finely chopped fresh
    chives, plus extra to garnish
  10ml/2 tsp finely chopped fresh basil
  15ml/1 tbsp finely chopped
    fresh parsley
  15ml/1 tbsp single (light) cream
  15ml/1 tbsp mayonnaise
  30ml/2 tbsp salad cream or
    extra mayonnaise
  5ml/1 tsp mild mustard
  2.5ml/½ tsp sugar

1 Cook the potatoes in a large pan of salted boiling water until tender but still firm. Drain and cool, then cut into 2.5cm/1in cubes and place in a large salad bowl.

COOK'S TIP
It is best to use waxy new potatoes for this dish, as older, floury ones may crumble or break up when boiled.

2 Cut the red peppers in half, cut away and discard the core and seeds, then cut into small pieces. Finely chop the celery, shallot and spring onions. Slice the chilli very thinly, discarding the seeds. Add the vegetables to the potatoes, with the garlic and chopped chives, basil and parsley.

3 Mix the cream, mayonnaise, salad cream or extra mayonnaise, mustard and sugar together in a small bowl. Stir until the mixture is well combined.

4 Pour the dressing over the potato and vegetable salad and stir gently to coat all the ingredients evenly. Garnish the salad with the extra chives just before it is served.

MANGO, TOMATO AND RED ONION SALAD

THIS SALAD MAKES A DELICIOUS APPETIZER AND IS OFTEN EATEN ON THE ISLANDS OF THE CARIBBEAN. UNDER-RIPE MANGO CONTRIBUTES A SUBTLE SWEETNESS THAT GOES WELL WITH THE TOMATO.

SERVES FOUR

INGREDIENTS
1 firm under-ripe mango
2 large tomatoes or 1 beefsteak
  tomato, sliced
½ cucumber, peeled and
  thinly sliced
½ red onion, sliced into rings
1 garlic clove, crushed
30ml/2 tbsp sunflower or
  vegetable oil
15ml/1 tbsp lemon juice
2.5ml/½ tsp hot pepper sauce
salt and ground black pepper
sugar, to taste
chopped chives, to garnish

1 Using a sharp knife, cut a thick slice or "cheek" from either side of the mango stone. Peel away the skin and slice the flesh into thin strips. Peel the remaining mango, remove the rest of the flesh and slice it thinly.

2 Arrange a layer of tomato slices on a large serving plate or platter. Top with the cucumber slices, followed by the mango, and finish off with the thin slices of red onion.

3 Make the salad dressing. Crush the garlic clove into a small glass bowl. Add the oil, lemon juice, hot pepper sauce, salt, ground black pepper and sugar, if you like. Using a balloon whisk or a fork, whisk these ingredients together until thoroughly mixed.

4 Drizzle the dressing evenly over the salad and garnish with chopped chives. Serve immediately.

COOK'S TIP
Choose the freshest, ripest tomatoes available for the best flavour.

SIDE DISHES AND GRAINS

Traditionally, Caribbean meals consist of a meat, poultry or fish dish accompanied by rice, beans or potatoes and a combination of side dishes, such as Rice and Peas, or stir-fried vegetables. Flat breads known as roti are often served with a meal for mopping up sauces. Other breads are made with corn meal instead of wheat flour.

RICE <u>AND</u> PEAS

IT MAY SEEM ODD THAT A DISH WITH KIDNEY BEANS AS A PRIMARY INGREDIENT IS CALLED RICE AND PEAS, BUT IN JAMAICA, WHERE IT ORIGINATED, FRESH PIGEON PEAS WERE ORIGINALLY USED. SINCE THE PEAS ARE SEASONAL, THE DISH IS MORE OFTEN MADE WITH DRIED KIDNEY BEANS.

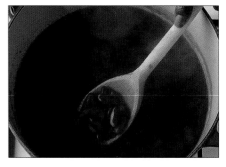

2 Drain the beans and tip them into a large pan with a tight-fitting lid. Pour in enough water to cover the beans. Bring to the boil and boil for 10 minutes, then lower the heat and simmer for 1½ hours or until the beans are tender.

3 Add the thyme, creamed coconut or coconut cream, bay leaves, onion, garlic, allspice and pepper. Season and stir in the measured water.

SERVES SIX

INGREDIENTS

200g/7oz/1 cup red kidney beans
2 fresh thyme sprigs
50g/2oz piece of creamed coconut or
  120ml/4fl oz/½ cup coconut cream
2 bay leaves
1 onion, finely chopped
2 garlic cloves, crushed
2.5ml/½ tsp ground allspice
1 red or green (bell) pepper, seeded
  and chopped
600ml/1 pint/2½ cups water
450g/1lb/2½ cups long grain rice
salt and ground black pepper

1 Put the red kidney beans in a large bowl. Pour in enough cold water to cover the beans generously. Cover the bowl and leave the beans to soak overnight.

4 Bring to the boil and add the rice. Stir well, reduce the heat and cover the pan. Simmer for 25–30 minutes, until all the liquid has been absorbed. Serve as an accompaniment to fish, meat or vegetarian dishes.

COU-COU

THIS TASTY OKRA AND MASHED CORN MEAL PUDDING IS A BAJAN NATIONAL DISH. TRADITIONALLY, IT IS SERVED WITH FRESH FLYING FISH COOKED IN A CARIBBEAN GRAVY, BUT IT CAN ALSO BE SERVED WITH ANY OTHER FISH, MEAT OR VEGETABLE STEW.

SERVES FOUR

INGREDIENTS
    115g/4oz okra, trimmed and
      roughly chopped
    225g/8oz/1½ cups coarse corn meal
    600ml/1 pint/2½ cups water or
      coconut milk
    25g/1oz/2 tbsp butter
    salt and ground black pepper

COOK'S TIP
Adding unsweetened coconut milk instead of water will give your cou-cou a special, rich flavour.

3 Cook on a very low heat, beating the mixture vigorously. Gradually add the measured water or coconut milk, beating after each addition to prevent the mixture from sticking to the pan and burning.

4 Cover and cook for about 20 minutes, beating occasionally. The cou-cou is cooked when the corn meal granules are soft. Cover with foil and then a lid to keep the mixture moist and hot until required. Spread with butter before serving.

1 Bring a pan of water seasoned with a little salt and pepper to the boil. Add the chopped okra and cook for about 10 minutes. Remove the okra with a slotted spoon and set it aside.

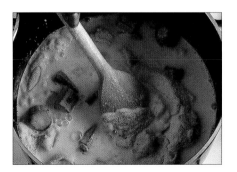

2 Pour away half the liquid from the pan, then return the pan to the heat. Return the okra to the pan, then gradually beat in the corn meal.

BUTTERED SPINACH AND RICE

THE LAYER OF FRESH COOKED SPINACH IN THIS POPULAR CARIBBEAN DISH IS SAID TO HAVE BEEN THE RESULT OF A HAPPY ACCIDENT. IT WAS INTENDED FOR A SEPARATE DISH, BUT THE COOK FORGOT TO ADD IT SO SIMPLY USED IT TO TOP THE RICE INSTEAD.

SERVES FOUR

INGREDIENTS
    40g/1½oz/3 tbsp butter or margarine
    1 onion, finely chopped
    2 fresh tomatoes, chopped
    450g/1lb/2½ cups basmati
        rice, rinsed
    2 garlic cloves, crushed
    600ml/1 pint/2½ cups stock or water
    350g/12oz fresh spinach, shredded
    salt and ground black pepper
    2 tomatoes, sliced, to garnish

COOK'S TIP
If you are unable to get fresh spinach, use frozen leaf spinach instead. Thaw and drain approximately 225g/8oz frozen spinach and cook on top of the rice for about 5 minutes. If you prefer, finely shredded spring greens (collards) make a delicious alternative to spinach.

1 Melt 25g/1oz/2 tbsp of butter or margarine in a large pan with a tight-fitting lid. Gently fry the onion for 3–4 minutes, until soft and translucent. Stir in the fresh chopped tomatoes.

2 Add the basmati rice and crushed garlic, gently cook for 5 minutes, then gradually add the stock or water, stirring constantly. Season to taste with plenty of salt and ground black pepper.

3 Cover and simmer gently for 10–15 minutes, until the rice is almost cooked, then reduce the heat to low.

4 Spread the spinach in a thick layer over the rice. Cover the pan and cook over a low heat for 5–8 minutes, until the spinach has wilted. Spoon into a serving dish, dot the remaining butter over the top and garnish with the sliced tomatoes. Serve immediately.

CREAMED SWEET POTATOES

SIMILAR TO TRADITIONAL MASHED POTATOES, THIS CARIBBEAN SPECIALITY USES WHITE SWEET POTATOES INSTEAD OF THE ORANGE VARIETY. THE GRATED NUTMEG ADDS AN EXTRA, IRRESISTIBLE SWEETNESS.

SERVES FOUR

INGREDIENTS
    900g/2lb sweet potatoes
    50g/2oz/¼ cup butter
    45ml/3 tbsp single (light) cream
    freshly grated nutmeg
    15ml/1 tbsp chopped fresh chives
    salt and ground black pepper

COOK'S TIP
If you cannot get white sweet potatoes, white yams make a good substitute, especially poona (Ghanaian) yam.

1 Peel the sweet potatoes under cold running water and place in a bowl of salted water to prevent them from discolouring. Cut them into large chunks and place in a pan of cold water. Cook, covered, for 20–30 minutes until tender.

2 Drain the potatoes and return them to the dry pan. Add the butter, cream, nutmeg, chives and seasoning. Mash with a potato masher and then fluff up with a fork. Serve warm as an accompaniment to a curry or stew.

OKRA FRIED RICE

OKRA WAS INTRODUCED TO MAINLAND SOUTH AMERICA AND THE ISLANDS OF THE CARIBBEAN BY THE AFRICAN SLAVES WHO WERE BROUGHT OVER TO WORK THE SUGAR PLANTATIONS. IT BECAME AN IMPORTANT AND MUCH-VALUED INGREDIENT.

SERVES FOUR

INGREDIENTS
  15ml/1 tbsp butter or margarine
  30ml/2 tbsp vegetable oil
  1 garlic clove, crushed
  ½ red onion, finely chopped
  115g/4oz okra, trimmed
  30ml/2 tbsp diced green and red
    (bell) peppers
  2.5ml/½ tsp dried thyme
  2 fresh green chillies, finely chopped
  2.5ml/½ tsp five-spice powder
  1 vegetable stock (bouillon) cube
  30ml/2 tbsp soy sauce
  15ml/1 tbsp chopped fresh
    coriander (cilantro)
  225g/8oz/2 cups cooked long grain
    white rice
  salt and ground black pepper
  fresh coriander, to garnish

1 Melt the butter or margarine in the oil in a frying pan or wok. Add the garlic and onion, and cook over a medium heat for 5 minutes, until the onion is soft but not browned.

2 Trim the okra, cutting off the stalks and points, then thinly slice the pods. Add to the pan or wok and cook gently for 6–7 minutes.

3 Add the green and red peppers, thyme, chillies and five-spice powder. Cook for 3 minutes, then crumble in the stock cube.

4 Add the soy sauce, chopped coriander and rice, and heat through, stirring well. Season with salt and pepper. Spoon into a dish and serve hot, garnished with the coriander sprigs.

AUBERGINES WITH GARLIC AND SPRING ONIONS

THIS IS A SUPERB WAY OF SERVING AUBERGINES. IT CAN BE MADE EVEN MORE DELICIOUS BY ADDING LITTLE STRIPS OF SMOKED SALMON AT THE LAST MINUTE AND LETTING THEM JUST WARM THROUGH.

SERVES FOUR

INGREDIENTS
  45ml/3 tbsp vegetable oil
  2 garlic cloves, crushed
  3 tomatoes, peeled and chopped
  900g/2lb aubergines (eggplants),
    cut into chunks
  150ml/¼ pint/⅔ cup vegetable
    stock or water
  30ml/2 tbsp soy sauce
  60ml/4 tbsp chopped spring
    onion (scallion)
  ½ red (bell) pepper, seeded
    and chopped
  1 fresh hot chilli, seeded
    and chopped
  30ml/2 tbsp chopped fresh
    coriander (cilantro)
  salt and ground black pepper

1 Heat the oil in a wok or frying pan and fry the garlic and tomatoes for 3–4 minutes. Add the aubergines and toss with the garlic and tomatoes.

2 Pour in the stock or water and cover the pan. Simmer gently until the aubergines are very soft. Stir in the soy sauce and half of the spring onion.

3 Add the red pepper and chilli to the aubergine. Season with salt and pepper to taste. Mix well.

4 Stir in the coriander and sprinkle with the remaining spring onion. Spoon the aubergine mixture into a dish and serve at once. Alternatively, allow to cool until warm before serving.

CORN STICKS

*This traditional Caribbean recipe produces perfect corn bread in a loaf tin.
Alternatively, if you can find the moulds, it can be used to make attractive corn sticks.*

MAKES FORTY

INGREDIENTS
    225g/8oz/2 cups plain
      (all-purpose) flour
    225g/8oz/2 cups fine corn meal
    50ml/10 tsp bicarbonate of soda
      (baking soda)
    2.5ml/½ tsp salt
    60ml/4 tbsp demerara (raw) sugar
    450ml/¾ pint/scant 2 cups milk
    2 eggs
    50g/2oz/4 tbsp butter or margarine

COOK'S TIP
Because there is such a lot of
bicarbonate of soda used in this recipe,
the corn meal mixture begins to rise as
soon as the liquid is added, so make
sure you bake straight away.

1 Preheat the oven to 190°C/375°F/
Gas 5 and grease either corn bread
moulds, if you can find them, or a
900g/2lb loaf tin (pan).

2 Sift together the flour, corn meal,
bicarbonate of soda, salt and sugar into
a large bowl. In a separate bowl, whisk
the milk and eggs, then stir into the
flour mixture.

3 Melt the butter or margarine in a
small pan and stir gradually into the
corn meal mixture.

4 Carefully spoon the thick mixture into
the moulds or tin. Bake the corn sticks
for about 15 minutes. If using a loaf tin,
you will need to bake for around 30–35
minutes, until the corn bread is golden
and hollow sounding when tapped.

FRIED YELLOW PLANTAINS

WHEN PLANTAINS ARE YELLOW IT IS A SIGN THAT THEY ARE RIPE. THEY ARE OFTEN ADDED TO MEAT, FISH OR VEGETARIAN DISHES IN THE CARIBBEAN, OR SERVED AS A TASTY ACCOMPANIMENT.

SERVES FOUR

INGREDIENTS
 2 yellow plantains
 oil, for shallow frying
 finely chopped chives, to garnish

1 Using a small sharp knife, trim the tops and tails of each plantain, then cut them in half.

2 Slit the skin along the natural ridges of each piece of plantain, and ease up using the tip of your thumb.

3 Peel away the entire plantain skin and discard. Thinly slice the plantains lengthways.

4 Heat a little oil in a frying pan and fry the plantain slices for 2–3 minutes on each side, until they are golden brown.

5 When the plantains are brown and crisp, drain on kitchen paper and serve sprinkled with chives.

COOK'S TIP
For the sweetest flavour, these gently fried plantain slices should be made using the ripest plantains available. The darker the skin, the riper the plantains are.

DHAL PURI

KNOWN AS ROTIS *IN THEIR NATIVE* INDIA, *THESE TASTY FLAT BREADS CAN ALSO BE MADE WITH WHITE FLOUR. A TRADITIONAL* CARIBBEAN *FAVOURITE,* DHAL PURI *ARE DELICIOUS WITH MEAT, FISH OR VEGETABLE DISHES AND ARE IDEAL FOR MOPPING UP LEFTOVER SAUCES.*

MAKES ABOUT FIFTEEN

INGREDIENTS
  450g/1lb/4 cups self-raising
    (self-rising) flour
  115g/4oz/1 cup wholemeal
    (whole-wheat) flour
  350ml/12fl oz/1½ cups cold water
  30ml/2 tbsp oil, plus extra for frying
  salt, to taste
For the filling
  350g/12oz/1½ cups yellow split peas
  15ml/1 tbsp ground cumin
  2 garlic cloves, crushed

1 Sift the dry ingredients into a bowl, then tip in the grain remaining in the sieve. Add the water a little at a time, and knead gently until a soft dough forms. Continue kneading until supple, but do not over-work the dough.

2 Add the oil to the dough and continue to knead it until it is completely smooth. Put the dough in a plastic bag or wrap in clear film (plastic wrap). Place in a cool room or in the refrigerator and leave to rest for at least 30 minutes, or overnight if possible.

3 To make the filling, put the split peas in a large pan, pour over water to cover and cook for about 10–15 minutes, until half cooked – they should be tender on the outside, but still firm in the middle. Allow the water to evaporate during cooking, until the pan is almost dry, but add a little extra water to prevent burning, if necessary.

4 Spread out the peas on a tray. When cool, grind to a paste, using a mortar and pestle or food processor. Mix with the cumin and garlic.

5 Divide the dough into about 15 balls, Slightly flatten each ball, put about 15ml/1 tbsp of the split pea mixture into the centre and fold over the edges.

6 Dust a rolling pin and a board with flour and roll out the *dhal puri*, taking care not to overstretch the dough, until they are about 18cm/7in in diameter.

7 Heat a little oil in a frying pan. Cook the *dhal puris* for about 3 minutes on each side until light brown. Serve as soon as the last one is cooked.

FRIED DUMPLINS

In the Caribbean these fried dumplins are simply called "bakes". They are usually served with salt fish or fried fish, but can be eaten quite simply with butter and jam or cheese, which children especially love.

MAKES ABOUT TEN

INGREDIENTS
  450g/1lb/4 cups self-raising
    (self-rising) flour
  10ml/2 tsp sugar
  2.5ml/½ tsp salt
  300ml/½ pint/1¼ cups milk
  oil, for frying

COOK'S TIP
Mix and knead the dough gently to avoid overworking it and making it tough. A quite light touch is all that is needed to make the dough smooth.

1 Sift the flour, sugar and salt into a large bowl, add the milk and mix and knead until a smooth dough forms.

2 Divide the dough into ten balls, kneading each ball with floured hands. Press the balls gently to flatten them into 7.5cm/3in rounds.

3 Heat a little oil in a non-stick frying pan over medium heat. Place half the dumplins in the pan, reduce the heat to low and fry for about 15 minutes, until they are golden brown, turning once.

4 Stand the dumplins on their sides for a few minutes to brown the edges, before removing them from the pan and draining thoroughly on kitchen paper. Serve immediately, while still warm.

PIGEON PEAS COOK-UP RICE

THIS RICE DISH IS MADE WITH THE MOST COMMONLY USED PEAS. IT MAKES AN EXCELLENT ACCOMPANIMENT TO ANY MEAT, POULTRY OR FISH MEAL.

SERVES FOUR TO SIX

INGREDIENTS

25g/1oz/2 tbsp butter or margarine
1 medium onion, chopped
1 garlic clove, chopped
25g/1oz/2 tbsp chopped spring
  onion (scallion)
1 large carrot, diced
175g/6oz/1 cup pigeon peas
1 thyme sprig or 5ml/1 tsp dried thyme
1 cinnamon stick
600ml/1pint/2½ cups vegetable stock
100ml/3½ fl oz/scant ½ cup
  coconut cream
1 hot chilli pepper, chopped
450g/1lb long grain rice
salt and ground black pepper

1 Melt the butter or margarine in a large heavy pan, add the onion and garlic and sauté over a medium heat for 5 minutes, stirring occasionally.

2 Add the spring onion, carrot, pigeon peas, thyme, cinnamon, stock, creamed coconut, hot pepper and seasoning and bring to the boil.

3 Reduce the heat and then stir in the rice. Cover and simmer gently, over a low heat, until all the liquid is absorbed and the rice is tender.

4 Stir with a fork to fluff up the rice before serving.

COOK'S TIP
Pigeon peas are also known as gunga peas. The fresh peas can be difficult to obtain, but you will find them in specialist shops. The frozen peas are green and the canned variety are brown, Drain the salted water from canned peas and rinse before using them in this recipe.

GREEN BANANAS AND YAM IN COCONUT MILK

THIS SIDE DISH HAS ALL THE FLAVOURS OF THE CARIBBEAN – COCONUT, GREEN BANANA AND YAM. IT'S VERY EASY TO MAKE AND PARTICULARLY POPULAR WITH CHILDREN.

SERVES THREE TO FOUR

INGREDIENTS

3 green bananas, peeled and halved
450g/1lb white yam, peeled and cut
  into bitesize pieces
1 thyme sprig
75ml/2½ fl oz/⅓ cup coconut cream
salt and ground black pepper
chopped fresh thyme, and thyme
  sprigs, to garnish

COOK'S TIP
Yams have either yellow or white flesh – the white variety is needed for this recipe. Some yams are huge, so when buying ask for a piece the size you need. Yams and green bananas are available in specialist food stores.

1 Bring 900ml/1½ pints/3¾ cups water to the boil in a large pan, reduce the heat and add the green bananas and yam. Simmer gently for 10 minutes.

2 Add the thyme, coconut and seasoning, bring back to the boil and cook over a moderate heat until tender.

3 Transfer the yam and banana to a plate and continue cooking the coconut milk until thick and creamy.

4 When the sauce is ready, return vegetables to the pan and heat through. To serve, sprinkle with chopped thyme and garnish with thyme sprigs.

DESSERTS AND DRINKS

The abundant supply of sweet and juicy tropical fruit in the Caribbean means that dessert usually consists of fresh fruit. Otherwise, desserts tend to be rice or tapioca dishes, based on egg and sugar, ice cream or cakes. The Caribbean is famous for its cocktails, which are usually based on rum with the addition of fresh fruit or juices, and a little spice.

FRUITS OF THE TROPICS SALAD

CANNED GUAVAS DO NOT HAVE QUITE THE SAME FLAVOUR AS FRESH ONES, BUT ARE AN EXCELLENT
INGREDIENT IN THEIR OWN RIGHT — DELICIOUS IN THIS CARIBBEAN FRUIT SALAD.

2 Chop the stem ginger and add it to the pineapple mixture.

3 Pour the ginger syrup into a blender or food processor. Add the remaining banana, the coconut milk and the sugar. Pour in the reserved guava syrup and blend to a smooth creamy purée.

SERVES SIX

INGREDIENTS

  1 medium pineapple
  400g/14oz can guava halves in syrup
  2 bananas, sliced
  1 large mango, peeled, stoned
   (pitted) and diced
  115g/4oz preserved stem ginger
   plus 30ml/2 tbsp of the syrup from
   the jar
  60ml/4 tbsp thick coconut milk
  10ml/2 tsp sugar
  2.5ml/½ tsp freshly grated nutmeg
  2.5ml/½ tsp ground cinnamon
  strips of coconut, to decorate

1 Remove the leafy top of the pineapple, saving it to decorate the serving platter if you like. Cut the pineapple lengthways into quarters, then remove the peel and core from each piece. Cube the pineapple, and place in a serving bowl. Drain the guavas, reserving the syrup, and chop. Add the guavas to the bowl with half the bananas and all the mango.

4 Pour the banana and coconut dressing over the fruit, add a little grated nutmeg and a sprinkling of cinnamon. Cover and chill.

5 Serve the salad chilled, decorated with fresh strips of coconut. If you are serving the mixture on a large platter, the pineapple top can be placed in the centre as a decoration.

COCONUT ICE CREAM

THIS HEAVENLY ICE CREAM, POPULAR THROUGHOUT THE CARIBBEAN, IS EASY TO MAKE AND USES STORECUPBOARD INGREDIENTS, SO IS PERFECT FOR EASY ENTERTAINING.

SERVES EIGHT

INGREDIENTS
    400g/14oz can evaporated
      (unsweetened condensed) milk
    400g/14oz can condensed milk
    400g/14oz can coconut milk
    freshly grated nutmeg
    5ml/1 tsp almond essence (extract)
    fresh lemon balm sprigs, lime slices
      and shredded coconut, to decorate

COOK'S TIP
If using an ice-cream maker, mix the ingredients in a jug (pitcher), chill in the freezer for 30 minutes. Pour into the ice-cream maker and churn as directed.

3 Remove the bowl from the freezer and whisk the mixture vigorously until it is light and fluffy and has almost doubled in volume.

4 Pour into a freezer container, then cover and freeze. Soften slightly before serving, decorated with lemon balm, lime slices and shredded coconut.

1 Mix the evaporated, condensed and coconut milk in a large freezerproof bowl until thoroughly combined.

2 Stir in the grated nutmeg and almond essence. Place the bowl in the freezer and chill the mixture for about 1–2 hours or until semi-frozen.

TAPIOCA PUDDING

THIS IS ONE OF THOSE DESSERTS THAT PROVOKES STRONG REACTIONS. MOST PEOPLE EITHER LOVE IT OR LOATHE IT, BUT IT IS VERY POPULAR THROUGHOUT THE CARIBBEAN. FOR ITS MANY FANS, THERE IS NOTHING NICER THAN THIS CREAMY DESSERT STREWN WITH CRUNCHY CASHEWS.

SERVES SIX

INGREDIENTS
90g/3½oz/generous ½ cup tapioca
750ml/1¼ pints/3 cups full-fat
  (whole) milk
1 cinnamon stick, bruised
45ml/3 tbsp caster (superfine) sugar
30ml/2 tbsp chopped cashew nuts

1 Put the tapioca in a strainer and rinse under cold running water. Drain and tip into a heavy pan.

VARIATION
For coconut-flavoured tapioca pudding, simply replace the milk with the same quantity of coconut milk.

2 Pour in the milk and soak for 30 minutes. Place the pan over a medium heat and bring to the boil. Add the bruised cinnamon stick, then lower the heat and simmer gently for 30 minutes, or until most of the milk has been absorbed. Stir occasionally to prevent the tapioca from sticking.

3 Stir in the sugar and gently simmer for a further 10 minutes. Carefully remove the cinnamon stick and spoon the pudding into individual dessert bowls. Lightly toast the cashew nuts in a dry frying pan, taking care not to burn them, and scatter over the puddings. Serve warm rather than hot or cold.

FRIED BANANAS WITH SUGAR AND RUM

CHILDREN LOVE FRIED BANANAS, BUT THIS CARIBBEAN VERSION WITH RUM DELIVERS AN EXTRA KICK AND IS STRICTLY FOR GROWN-UPS. FRIED BANANAS CAN BE INCREDIBLY SWEET, BUT THE LIME JUICE CUTS THROUGH THE SWEETNESS WITH DELICIOUS RESULTS.

SERVES FOUR

INGREDIENTS
    50g/2oz/¼ cup caster
      (superfine) sugar
    45ml/3 tbsp rum
    65g/2½oz/5 tbsp unsalted
      (sweet) butter
    grated rind and juice of 1 lime
    4 bananas, peeled
    vanilla ice cream, to serve

1 Place the sugar, rum, butter, grated lime rind and lime juice in a large heavy frying pan over a low heat. Cook for a few minutes, stirring occasionally, until the sugar has completely dissolved.

COOK'S TIP
Avoid using bananas that are too ripe, otherwise they may break apart in the pan before they get a chance to colour.

2 Add the bananas to the pan, turning to coat them in the sauce. Cook over a medium heat for 5 minutes on each side, or until the bananas are golden.

3 Remove from the heat and cut the bananas in half. Serve two pieces of banana per person with a scoop of vanilla ice cream and a generous drizzle of the hot sauce.

CARIBBEAN SPICED RICE PUDDING

SOME RECIPES FROM THE CARIBBEAN CAN BE EXTREMELY SWEET, PARTICULARLY DESSERTS. IF THIS RICE PUDDING IS A LITTLE TOO SWEET FOR YOUR TASTE, SIMPLY REDUCE THE SUGAR QUANTITY AND RELY UPON THE NATURAL SWEETNESS OF THE FRUIT.

SERVES SIX

INGREDIENTS
   25g/1oz/2 tbsp butter
   1 cinnamon stick
   115g/4oz/½ cup soft brown sugar
   115g/4oz/⅔ cup ground rice
   1.2 litres/2 pints/5 cups milk
   2.5ml/½ tsp allspice
   50g/2oz/⅓ cup sultanas (golden
      raisins)
   75g/3oz mandarin oranges, chopped
   75g/3oz pineapple, chopped

1 Melt the butter in a non-stick pan. Add the cinnamon stick and sugar. Heat over a medium heat until the sugar just begins to caramelize. Remove from the heat.

2 Carefully stir in the rice and three-quarters of the milk. Slowly bring to the boil, stirring all the time, being careful not to let the milk burn. Reduce the heat and simmer gently for about 10 minutes, or until the rice is cooked, stirring constantly.

3 Add the remaining milk, the allspice and the sultanas. Leave to simmer for 5 minutes, stirring occasionally.

4 When the rice is thick and creamy, allow to cool slightly, then stir in the mandarin and pineapple pieces.

JAMAICAN FRUIT TRIFLE

THIS TRIFLE IS ACTUALLY BASED ON A CARIBBEAN FOOL THAT CONSISTS OF FRUIT STIRRED INTO THICK VANILLA-FLAVOURED CREAM. THIS VERSION IS MUCH LESS RICH, REDRESSING THE BALANCE WITH PLENTY OF FRUIT, AND WITH CRÈME FRAÎCHE REPLACING SOME OF THE CREAM.

SERVES EIGHT

INGREDIENTS

  1 large pineapple, peeled and cored
  300ml/½ pint/1¼ cups double
   (heavy) cream
  200ml/7fl oz/scant 1 cup crème fraîche
  60ml/4 tbsp icing (confectioners')
   sugar, sifted
  10ml/2 tsp pure vanilla essence
   (extract)
  30ml/2 tbsp white or coconut rum
  3 papayas, peeled, seeded and chopped
  3 mangoes, peeled, stoned (pitted)
   and chopped
  thinly pared rind and juice of 1 lime
  25g/1oz/⅓ cup coarsely shredded or
   flaked coconut, toasted

1 Cut the pineapple into large chunks, place in a food processor or blender and process briefly until chopped. Tip into a sieve placed over a bowl and leave for 5 minutes so that most of the juice drains from the fruit.

2 Whip the double cream to soft peaks, then fold in the crème fraîche, sifted icing sugar, vanilla extract and rum.

3 Fold the drained chopped pineapple into the cream mixture. Place the chopped papayas and mangoes in a large bowl and pour over the lime juice. Gently stir the fruit mixture to combine. Shred the pared lime rind.

4 Divide the fruit mixture and the pineapple cream among eight dessert plates. Decorate with the lime shreds, toasted coconut and a few small pineapple leaves, if you like, and serve at once.

COOK'S TIP
It is important to let the pineapple purée drain thoroughly, otherwise, the pineapple cream will be watery. Don't throw away the drained pineapple juice – mix it with fizzy mineral water for a refreshing drink.

CARIBBEAN FRUIT AND RUM CAKE

THIS POPULAR CAKE IS EATEN AT CHRISTMAS, WEDDINGS AND OTHER SPECIAL OCCASIONS. IT IS KNOWN AS BLACK CAKE, BECAUSE THE TRADITIONAL RECIPE USES BURNT SUGAR.

MAKES ONE CAKE

INGREDIENTS
  450g/1lb/2 cups currants
  450g/1lb/3 cups raisins
  225g/8oz/1 cup pitted prunes
  115g/4oz/⅔ cup mixed (candied) peel
  5ml/1 tsp ground mixed spice
   (pumpkin pie spice)
  90ml/6 tbsp rum, plus more
   if needed
  300ml/½ pint/1¼ cups sherry, plus
   more if needed
  400g/14oz/1¾ cups soft dark
   brown sugar
  450g/1lb/4 cups self-raising
   (self-rising) flour
  450g/1lb/2 cups butter, softened
  10 eggs, beaten
  5ml/1 tsp natural vanilla
   essence (extract)

1 Wash the currants, raisins, prunes and mixed peel, then drain and pat dry. Place in a food processor and process until roughly chopped. Transfer to a large, bowl and add the the mixed spice, rum and sherry. Stir in 115g/4oz/½ cup of sugar. Mix well, then cover with a lid and set aside for anything from 2 weeks to 3 months – the longer it is left, the better the flavour will be.

2 Stir the fruit mixture occasionally, adding more alcohol, if you like, before replacing the cover.

3 Preheat the oven to 160ºC/325ºF/ Gas 3. Grease a 25cm/10in round cake tin (pan) and line with a double layer of greaseproof (waxed) paper or baking parchment.

4 Sift the flour into a bowl, and set it aside. In a large mixing bowl, cream the butter with the remaining sugar. Beat in the eggs until the mixture is smooth and creamy, adding a little of the flour if the mixture starts to curdle.

5 Add the fruit mixture, then gradually stir in the remaining flour and the vanilla essence. Mix well, adding 15–30ml/1–2 tbsp more sherry if the mixture is too stiff; it should just fall off the back of the spoon, but should not be too runny.

6 Spoon the mixture into the prepared pan, cover loosely with foil and bake for about 2½ hours, until the cake is firm and springy. Leave to cool in the pan overnight. Unless serving immediately, sprinkle the cake with more rum and wrap in greaseproof paper and foil to keep it moist.

COOK'S TIP
Although it is usual to roughly chop the dried fruits, they can be marinated whole if you prefer. If there is no time to marinate the fruit, simmer it gently in the alcohol mixture for about 30 minutes, and leave overnight.

APPLE AND CINNAMON CRUMBLE CAKE

THIS SCRUMPTIOUS CAKE, POPULAR IN THE CARIBBEAN, HAS LAYERS OF SPICY FRUIT AND CRUMBLE AND IS QUITE DELICIOUS WHEN SERVED WARM WITH FRESH CREAM.

MAKES ONE CAKE

INGREDIENTS
  250g/9oz/1 cup plus 30ml/2 tbsp
    butter, softened
  250g/9oz/1¼ cups caster
    (superfine) sugar
  4 eggs
  450g/1lb/4 cups self-raising
    (self-rising) flour
  3 large cooking apples
  2.5ml/½ tsp ground cinnamon
For the crumble topping
  175g/6oz/¾ cup demerara
    (raw) sugar
  125g/4¼oz/generous 1 cup plain
    (all-purpose) flour
  5ml/1 tsp ground cinnamon
  65g/2½oz/scant 1 cup desiccated
    (dry unsweetened shredded) coconut
  115g/4oz/½ cup butter

1 Preheat the oven to 180°C/350°F/ Gas 4. Grease and base-line a 25cm/ 10in round cake tin (pan). To make the crumble topping, mix the sugar, flour, cinnamon and coconut in a bowl, then rub in the butter with your fingertips until the mixture resembles breadcrumbs. Set aside.

2 Put the butter and sugar in a bowl and cream with an electric mixer until light and fluffy. Beat in the eggs, one at a time, beating well after each addition, and adding a little of the flour if the mixture starts to curdle.

3 Sift in half the remaining flour, mix well, then add the rest of the flour and stir until smooth.

4 Peel and core the apples, then grate them coarsely. Place the grated apples in a bowl and sprinkle with the cinnamon and set aside.

5 Spread half the cake mixture evenly over the base of the prepared tin. Spoon the apples on top and sprinkle over half the crumble topping.

6 Spread the remaining cake mixture over the crumble and finally top with the remaining crumble topping.

7 Bake for 1 hour 10 minutes–1 hour 20 minutes, covering the cake with foil if it browns too quickly. Leave in the pan for about 5 minutes before turning out on to a wire rack. Serve when cool.

BARBADIAN COCONUT SWEET BREAD

OFTEN MADE AT CHRISTMAS TIME IN BARBADOS, THIS DELICIOUS COCONUT BREAD IS MOST ENJOYABLE WITH A CUP OF HOT CHOCOLATE OR A GLASS OF FRUIT PUNCH.

MAKES TWO SMALL LOAVES

INGREDIENTS
  175g/6oz/¾ cup butter or margarine
  115g/4oz/½ cup demerara
    (raw) sugar
  225g/8oz/2 cups self-raising
    (self-rising) flour
  200g/7oz/scant 2 cups plain
    (all-purpose) flour
  115g/4oz desiccated (dry
    unsweetened shredded) coconut
  5ml/1 tsp mixed spice (pumpkin
    pie spice)
  10ml/2 tsp vanilla essence (extract)
  15ml/1 tbsp rum (optional)
  2 eggs
  about 150ml/¼ pint/⅔ cup milk
  15ml/1 tbsp caster (superfine)
    sugar, blended with 30ml/2 tbsp
    water, to glaze

1 Preheat the oven to 180°C/350°F/
Gas 4. Grease two 450g/1lb loaf tins
(pans) or one 900g/2lb tin.

2 Place the butter or margarine and
sugar in a large mixing bowl and sift
in all of the flour. Rub the ingredients
together with your fingertips until the
mixture begins to resemble fine
breadcrumbs.

3 Add the coconut, mixed spice, vanilla
essence, rum, if using, eggs and milk.
Mix together well with your hands. If the
mixture is too dry, add more milk. Knead
on a floured board until firm and pliable.

4 Halve the mixture and place in the
loaf tins. Glaze with sugared water and
bake for about 1 hour, or until a skewer
inserted into the loaf comes out clean.

DUCKANOO

THIS TASTY CARIBBEAN CAKE, WHICH HAS ITS ORIGINS IN WEST AFRICA, IS STEAMED IN FOIL PARCELS TO RETAIN MOISTURE. IT CONSISTS MAINLY OF CORN MEAL AND COCONUT AND IS DELICIOUS WITH FRESH CREAM.

MAKES SIX

INGREDIENTS
450g/1lb/3 cups fine corn meal
350g/12oz fresh coconut, chopped
600ml/1 pint/2½ cups fresh milk
115g/4oz currants or raisins
50g/2oz/¼ cup butter or margarine,
  melted
115g/4oz/½ cup demerara (raw) sugar
60ml/4 tbsp water
1.5ml/¼ tsp freshly grated nutmeg
2.5ml/½ tsp ground cinnamon
5ml/1 tsp vanilla essence (extract)

1 Place the corn meal in a large bowl. Blend the coconut and the milk in a blender or food processor until smooth. Stir the coconut mixture into the corn meal, then add all of the remaining ingredients and stir well.

2 Take 6 pieces of foil and fold into 13 x 15cm/5 x 6in pockets leaving an opening on one short side. Fold over the edges of the remaining sides tightly to ensure that they are well sealed. This will prevent liquid seeping in.

3 Put one or two spoonfuls of the corn meal mixture into each foil pocket and fold over the final edge of foil to seal tightly.

4 Place the foil pockets in a large pan of boiling water. Cover and simmer for about 45–60 minutes. Lift the pockets out of the water and carefully remove the foil. Serve the duckanoo alone or with fresh cream.

MOJITO

A REFRESHING CUBAN COCKTAIL, THIS INCORPORATES RUM, MINT AND LIME. TAKE YOUR TIME DRINKING IT AND THE FLAVOUR OF THE MINT WILL GRADUALLY INTENSIFY.

MAKES ONE

INGREDIENTS
    juice of 1 lime
    15ml/1 tbsp caster (superfine) sugar
    4 fresh mint sprigs
    75ml/5 tbsp white rum
    crushed ice
    90ml/6 tbsp soda water (club soda)

COOK'S TIPS
• If you don't have a refrigerator that delivers crushed ice or a blender with sufficiently tough blades, put the ice in a freezer bag, wrap it in a dishtowel and beat it with a rolling pin. Alternatively, process the ice in a blender or food processor briefly.
• Shaking the cocktail bruises the mint leaves, releasing their flavour. If you do not have a cocktail shaker, bruise the mint leaves by hand before adding them.

1 Mix the lime juice and sugar in a cocktail shaker and shake until the sugar has dissolved.

2 Add three of the mint sprigs, the rum and some crushed ice and shake vigorously. Pour into a tall glass, top with the soda water and decorate with the remaining mint.

CUBA LIBRE

THIS SIMPLE COCKTAIL HAS ALWAYS BEEN VERY POPULAR, BUT SINCE CASTRO TOOK POWER IN 1959 ITS NAME IS SEEN AS POLITICALLY INCORRECT. CUBAN EXILES HAVE SARCASTICALLY RENAMED IT MENTIRITA, MEANING "LITTLE LIE".

MAKES ONE

INGREDIENTS
    crushed ice
    45ml/3 tbsp white rum
    75ml/5 tbsp cola
    1 lime wedge, optional

COOK'S TIP
Rum is made by fermenting and distilling the thick brown liquid (molasses) that is left behind after extracting sugar from sugar cane.

1 Spoon the crushed ice into a tall glass and top with the white rum.

2 Pour in the cola and decorate with a wedge of lime. Serve immediately.

DEMERARA RUM PUNCH

THE INSPIRATION FOR THIS PUNCH CAME FROM THE RUM DISTILLERY AT PLANTATION DIAMOND ESTATE IN GUYANA, WHERE SOME OF THE FINEST RUM IN THE WORLD IS MADE, AND THE TANTALIZING AROMAS OF SUGAR CANE AND RUM PERVADE THE AIR.

SERVES FOUR

INGREDIENTS

150ml/¼ pint/⅔ cup orange juice
150ml/¼ pint/⅔ cup
   pineapple juice
150ml/¼ pint/⅔ cup mango juice
120ml/4fl oz/½ cup water
250ml/8fl oz/1 cup dark rum
a shake of angostura bitters
freshly grated nutmeg
25g/1oz/2 tbsp demerara
   (raw) sugar
1 small banana
1 large orange

1 Pour the orange, pineapple and mango juices into a large punch bowl. Stir in the water.

2 Add the rum, angostura bitters, nutmeg and sugar. Stir gently for a few minutes until the sugar has dissolved.

3 Slice the banana thinly and stir the slices gently into the punch.

4 Slice the orange and add to the punch. Chill and serve in tumblers with ice.

VARIATIONS
You can use white rum instead of dark, if you prefer. To make a stronger punch, simply add more rum.

CARIBBEAN CREAM STOUT PUNCH

THIS FAIRLY UNUSUAL PUNCH, MADE USING STOUT, CONDENSED MILK AND SHERRY, IS A WELL-KNOWN "PICK-ME-UP" THAT IS POPULAR ALL OVER THE CARIBBEAN. WITH A SWEET, HEADY AROMA OF VANILLA, IT SOOTHES AND REVIVES TIRED MINDS AND BODIES.

SERVES TWO

INGREDIENTS
475ml/16fl oz/2 cups stout
300ml/½ pint/1¼ cups evaporated
  (unsweetened condensed) milk
75ml/5 tbsp condensed milk
75ml/5 tbsp sherry
2 or 3 drops vanilla
  essence (extract)
freshly grated nutmeg

1 Mix together the stout, evaporated and condensed milks, sherry and vanilla essence in a blender or food processor, or whisk together in a large mixing bowl, until creamy.

2 Add a little grated nutmeg to the stout mixture and blend or whisk thoroughly again for a few minutes.

3 Chill for at least 45 minutes, or until really cold, before ladling into small glasses to serve.

NUTRITIONAL INFORMATION

The nutritional analysis below is per portion, unless otherwise stated.

p12 Plantain and Sweet Potato Chips
Energy 396Kcal/1658kJ; Protein 1.7g; Carbohydrate 51.5g, of which sugars 12.6g; Fat 21.7g, of which saturates 2.5g; Cholesterol 0mg; Calcium 11mg; Fibre 2.8g; Sodium 11mg

p12 Coconut King Prawns Energy 186Kcal/774kJ; Protein 11.2g; Carbohydrate 3.1g, of which sugars 2.6g; Fat 14.5g, of which saturates 8.4g; Cholesterol 182mg; Calcium 111mg; Fibre 1.7g; Sodium 443mg

p14 Cheesy Eggs Energy 167Kcal/693kJ; Protein 9.9g; Carbohydrate 0.1g, of which sugars 0.1g; Fat 14.2g, of which saturates 4.7g; Cholesterol 240mg; Calcium 108mg; Fibre 0g; Sodium 179mg

p15 Crab Cakes Energy 240Kcal/997kJ; Protein 5.9g; Carbohydrate 13.3g, of which sugars 8.9g; Fat 18.6g, of which saturates 8.7g; Cholesterol 58mg; Calcium 58mg; Fibre 2.8g; Sodium 197mg

p16 Spinach Patties Energy 168Kcal/703kJ; Protein 2.7g; Carbohydrate 16.9g, of which sugars 0.9g; Fat 10.4g, of which saturates 6.3g; Cholesterol 42mg; Calcium 59mg; Fibre 1g; Sodium 93mg.

p16 Salt Fish Fritters Energy 108Kcal/453kJ; Protein 5.8g; Carbohydrate 12.1g, of which sugars 0.4g; Fat 4.4g, of which saturates 0.6g; Cholesterol 20mg; Calcium 30mg; Fibre 0.5g; Sodium 53mg.

p18 Fish and Sweet Potato Soup Energy 125Kcal/528kJ; Protein 11.6g; Carbohydrate 16.7g, of which sugars 5.0g; Fat 1.7g, of which saturates 0.3g; Cholesterol 20mg; Calcium 44mg; Fibre 8.4g; Sodium 223mg

p18 Caribbean Vegetable Soup Energy 195Kcal/820kJ; Protein 3.8g; Carbohydrate 33.7g, of which sugars 16.0g; Fat 5.9g, of which saturates 3.4g; Cholesterol 13mg; Calcium 52mg; Fibre 3.4g; Sodium 62mg

p20 Beef and Cassava Soup Energy 332Kcal/1400kJ; Protein 27.3g; Carbohydrate 28.6g, of which sugars 8.7g; Fat 7.8g, of which saturates 3.1g; Cholesterol 78mg; Calcium 62mg; Fibre 2.4g; Sodium 295mg

p21 Lamb and Lentil Soup Energy 530Kcal/2225kJ; Protein 57.0g; Carbohydrate 35.2g, of which sugars

2.8g; Fat 18.8g, of which saturates 8.0g; Cholesterol 167mg; Calcium 57mg; Fibre 3.0g; Sodium 180mg

p22 Creamy Spinach Soup Energy 323Kcal/1331kJ; Protein 8.2g; Carbohydrate 6.5g, of which sugars 5.9g; Fat 29.5g, of which saturates 20g; Cholesterol 55mg; Calcium 362mg; Fibre 3.8g; Sodium 300mg

p23 Split Pea and Pumpkin Soup Energy 207Kcal/881kJ; Protein 14.8g; Carbohydrate 36.7g, of which sugars 5.7g; Fat 1.2g, of which saturates 0.3g; Cholesterol 0mg; Calcium 71mg; Fibre 4.7g; Sodium 30mg

p26 Salmon in Mango and Ginger Sauce Energy 718Kcal/2999kJ; Protein 56.8g; Carbohydrate 32.6g, of which sugars 32.3g; Fat 40.9g, of which saturates 11.9g; Cholesterol 164mg; Calcium 79mg; Fibre 2.5g; Sodium 359mg

p26 Fried Snapper with Avocado Energy 294Kcal/1223kJ; Protein 27.0g; Carbohydrate 0.9g, of which sugars 0.3g; Fat 20.2g, of which saturates 3.5g; Cholesterol 90mg; Calcium 31mg; Fibre 1.7g; Sodium 146mg

p28 Trout in Wine Sauce with Plantain Energy 324Kcal/1353kJ; Protein 22.0g; Carbohydrate 17.6g, of which sugars 6.1g; Fat 16.2g, of which saturates 5.2g; Cholesterol 83mg; Calcium 28mg; Fibre 0.6g; Sodium 139g

p29 Eschovished Fish Energy 210Kcal/879kJ; Protein 28.0g; Carbohydrate 5.4g, of which sugars 4.7g; Fat 8.5g, of which saturates 1.1g; Cholesterol 69mg; Calcium 28mg; Fibre 0.8g; Sodium 91mg

p30 Pumpkin and Prawns with Dried Shrimp Energy 210Kcal/877kJ; Protein 17.5g; Carbohydrate 8.7g, of which sugars 6.9g; Fat 11.9g, of which saturates 4.3g; Cholesterol 187mg; Calcium 147mg; Fibre 3.0g; Sodium 1g

p31 Salt Fish and Ackee Energy 292Kcal/1225kJ; Protein 38.4g; Carbohydrate 7.7g, of which sugars 6.2g; Fat 12.2g, of which saturates 4.3g; Cholesterol 80mg; Calcium 78mg; Fibre 2.4g; Sodium 494mg

p32 Jamaican Fish Curry Energy 695Kcal/2921kJ; Protein 39.5g; Carbohydrate 69.7g, of which sugars 11.2g; Fat 30.7g, of which saturates 19.3g; Cholesterol 51mg; Calcium 112mg; Fibre 3.3g; Sodium 216mg

p34 Crab and Corn Gumbo Energy 274Kcal/1144kJ; Protein 9.8g; Carbohydrate 24.2g, of which sugars 6.8g; Fat 11.4g, of which saturates 4.1g; Cholesterol 31mg; Calcium 77mg; Fibre 3.4g; Sodium 349mg

p35 Creole Fish Stew Energy 172Kcal/724kJ; Protein 17.8g; Carbohydrate 5.8g, of which sugars 5.1g; Fat 8.7g, of which saturates 1.9g; Cholesterol 45.8mg; Calcium 59mg; Fibre 1.8g; Sodium 222mg

p36 Cuban Seafood Rice Energy 326Kcal/1379kJ; Protein 28.4g; Carbohydrate 40.9g, of which sugars 1.1g; Fat 6.6g, of which saturates 1.2g; Cholesterol 286mg; Calcium 112mg; Fibre 0.5g; Sodium 1.2g

p38 King Prawns in Sweetcorn Sauce Energy 195Kcal/821kJ; Protein 15.4g; Carbohydrate 17.9g, of which sugars 10g; Fat 7.4g, of which saturates 4.2g; Cholesterol 162mg; Calcium 92mg; Fibre 1.1g; Sodium 407mg

p38 Prawns and Salt Fish with Okra Energy 256Kcal/1073kJ; Protein 38.1g; Carbohydrate 3.9g, of which sugars 3.1g; Fat 9.9g, of which saturates 4.1g; Cholesterol 271mg; Calcium 274mg; Fibre 3.7g; Sodium 542mg

p42 Peppered Steak in Sherry Cream Sauce Energy 427Kcal/1780kJ; Protein 38.1g; Carbohydrate 8.4g, of which sugars 3.3g; Fat 23.3g, of which saturates 10.7g; Cholesterol 115mg; Calcium 40mg; Fibre 7.4g; Sodium 142mg

p43 Oxtail and Butter Beans Energy 773Kcal/3240kJ; Protein 88.0g; Carbohydrate 29.6g, of which sugars 6.2g; Fat 34.4g, of which saturates 0.2g; Cholesterol 275mg; Calcium 92mg; Fibre 4.8g; Sodium 522mg

p44 Pork Roasted wtih Herbs, Spices and Rum Energy 410Kcal/1712kJ; Protein 42.4g; Carbohydrate 3.9g, of which sugars 3.8g; Fat 21.4g, of which saturates 8.2g; Cholesterol 132mg; Calcium 16mg; Fibre 0.1g; Sodium 577mg

p45 Caribbean Lamb Curry Energy 338Kcal/1409kJ; Protein 30.8g; Carbohydrate 3.2g, of which sugars 2.3g; Fat 22.6g, of which saturates 10.1g; Cholesterol 128mg; Calcium 29mg; Fibre 0.5g; Sodium 229mg

p46 "Seasoned-up" Lamb in Spinach Sauce Energy 331Kcal/1380kJ; Protein 35.6g; Carbohydrate 4.0g, of which sugars 3.1g; Fat 19.4g, of which saturates 6.7g; Cholesterol 125mg; Calcium 80mg; Fibre 1g; Sodium 241mg

p46 Lamb Pelau Energy 652Kcal/2726kJ; Protein 32.1g; Carbohydrate 96.3g, of which sugars 5.7g; Fat 15.0g, of which saturates 7.3g; Cholesterol 97mg; Calcium 51mg; Fibre 1.0g; Sodium 231mg

p48 Barbecued Jerk Chicken Energy 460Kcal/1924kJ; Protein 59.7g; Carbohydrate 2.2g, of which sugars 2.2g; Fat 23.6g, of which saturates 6.4g; Cholesterol 254mg; Calcium 26mg; Fibre 0.0g; Sodium 0.21g

p49 Thyme and Lime Chicken Energy 495Kcal/2053kJ; Protein 31.6g; Carbohydrate 0.4g, of which sugars 0.4g; Fat 40.8g, of which saturates 16.7g; Cholesterol 212mg; Calcium 24mg; Fibre 0.1g; Sodium 0.25g

p50 Spicy Fried Chicken Energy 345Kcal/1442kJ; Protein 35.5g; Carbohydrate 6.7g, of which sugars 1.0g; Fat 19.8g, of which saturates 4.5g; Cholesterol 177g; Calcium 54mg; Fibre 0.2g; Sodium 0.17g

p51 Sunday Roast Chicken Energy 348Kcal/1455kJ; Protein 37.5g; Carbohydrate 7.8g, of which sugars 7.8g; Fat 18.8g, of which saturates 8.8g; Cholesterol 155mg; Calcium 18mg; Fibre 0.0g; Sodium 200mg

p52 Peanut Chicken Energy 326Kcal/1374kJ; Protein 55.5g; Carbohydrate 4.2g, of which sugars 3.1g; Fat 9.8g, of which saturates 4.5g; Cholesterol 171mg; Calcium 25mg; Fibre 0.9g; Sodium 190mg

p53 Breast of Turkey with Mango and Wine Energy 351Kcal/1476kJ; Protein 49.9g; Carbohydrate 9.0g, of which sugars 6.4g; Fat 10.4g, of which saturates 6.0g; Cholesterol 135mg; Calcium 29mg; Fibre 1.5g; Sodium 190mg

p56 Macaroni Cheese Pie Energy 609Kcal/2553kJ; Protein 25.1g; Carbohydrate 60.0g, of which sugars 9.9g; Fat 31.6g, of which saturates 18.6g; Cholesterol 135mg; Calcium 494mg; Fibre 2.4g; Sodium 560mg

p57 Red Bean Chilli Energy 291Kcal/1224kJ; Protein 12.7g; Carbohydrate 35.7g, of which sugars 11.0g; Fat 6.5g, of which saturates 0.8g; Cholesterol 0mg; Calcium 86mg; Fibre 6.1g; Sodium 1.2g

p58 Spicy Vegetable Chow Mein Energy 414Kcal/1740kJ; Protein 12.4g; Carbohydrate 62.5g, of which sugars 8.5g; Fat 14.4g, of which saturates 2.7g; Cholesterol 23mg; Calcium 74mg; Fibre 4.7g; Sodium 266mg

p58 Aubergines Stuffed with Sweet Potato Energy 249Kcal/1013kJ; Protein 8.1g; Carbohydrate 24.6g, of which sugars 7.9g; Fat 13.1g, of which saturates 5.1g; Cholesterol 15mg; Calcium 186mg; Fibre 5.0g; Sodium 170mg

p60 Spinach Plantain Rounds Energy 266Kcal/1113kJ; Protein 5.9g; Carbohydrate 30.8g, of which sugars 7.6g; Fat 14.1g, of which saturates 3.6g; Cholesterol 65mg; Calcium 207mg; Fibre 3.6g; Sodium 205mg

p61 Peppery Bean Salad Energy 248Kcal/1046kJ; Protein 14.0g; Carbohydrate 35.4g, of which sugars 6.5g; Fat 6.5g, of which saturates 0.9g; Cholesterol 0mg; Calcium 122mg; Fibre 11.0g; Sodium 660mg

p62 Spicy Potato Salad Energy 184Kcal/ 776kJ; Protein 3.9g; Carbohydrate 30.0g, of which sugars 7.0g; Fat 6.2g, of which saturates 1.0g; Cholesterol 6mg; Calcium 32mg; Fibre 3.7g; Sodium 100mg

p63 Mango, Tomato and Red Onion Salad Energy 93Kcal/390kJ; Protein 1.0g; Carbohydrate 10.1g, of which sugars 9.5g; Fat 5.8g, of which saturates 0.7g; Cholesterol 0mg; Calcium 17mg; Fibre 2.1g; Sodium 6mg

p66 Rice and Peas Energy 449Kcal/ 1903kJ; Protein 13.9g; Carbohydrate 83.3g, of which sugars 4.4g; Fat 9.1g, of which saturates 5.7g; Cholesterol 0mg; Calcium 82mg; Fibre 6.3g; Sodium 10mg

p67 Cou-cou Energy 264Kcal/1115kJ; Protein 1.2g; Carbohydrate 52.7g, of which sugars 0.8g; Fat 6.8g, of which saturates 4.1g; Cholesterol 16mg; Calcium 56mg; Fibre 1.2g; Sodium 80mg

p68 Buttered Spinach and Rice Energy 520Kcal/2169kJ; Protein 11.5g; Carbohydrate 95.4g, of which sugars 4.6g; Fat 9.7g, of which saturates 5.3g; Cholesterol 21mg; Calcium 184mg; Fibre 2.7g; Sodium 190mg

p68 Creamed Sweet Potatoes Energy 313Kcal/1321kJ; Protein 4.4g; Carbohydrate 51.1g, of which sugars 13.4g; Fat 11.6g, of which saturates 6.8g; Cholesterol 27mg; Calcium 74mg; Fibre 9.6g; Sodium 170mg

p70 Okra Fried Rice Energy 305Kcal/ 1286kJ; Protein 4.7g; Carbohydrate 50.6g, of which sugars 1.9g; Fat 10.7g, of which saturates 3.1g; Cholesterol 8mg; Calcium 35mg; Fibre 0.5g; Sodium 65mg

p70 Aubergines with Garlic and Spring Onions Energy 132Kcal/551kJ; Protein 3.2g; Carbohydrate 9.3g, of which sugars 8.7g; Fat 9.5g, of which saturates 1.3g; Cholesterol 0mg; Calcium 36mg; Fibre 5.7g; Sodium 550mg

p72 Corn Sticks Energy 64Kcal/272kJ; Protein 1.4g; Carbohydrate 11.7g, of which sugars 1.9g; Fat 1.7g, of which saturates 0.9g; Cholesterol 15mg; Calcium 36mg; Fibre 0.2g; Sodium 160mg

p73 Fried Yellow Plantains Energy 267Kcal/1126kJ; Protein 1.5g; Carbohydrate 47.5g, of which sugars 11.5g; Fat 9.2g, of which saturates 1g; Cholesterol 0mg; Calcium 6mg; Fibre 2.3g; Sodium 0mg

p74 Dhal Puri Energy 237Kcal/1004kJ; Protein 9.2g; Carbohydrate 40.8g, of which sugars 1.1g; Fat 5.2g, of which saturates 0.6g; Cholesterol 0mg; Calcium 120mg; Fibre 2.8g; Sodium 120mg

p75 Fried Dumplins Energy 205Kcal/ 868kJ; Protein 5g; Carbohydrate 36.3g, of which sugars 2.8g; Fat 5.4g, of which saturates 0.9g; Cholesterol 2mg; Calcium 194mg; Fibre 1.4g; Sodium 270mg

p76 Pigeon Peas Cook-Up Rice Energy 199Kcal/827kJ; Protein 6.3g; Carbohydrate 14.2g, of which sugars 7g; Fat 13.4g, of which saturates 9.5g; Cholesterol 18mg; Calcium 67mg; Fibre 4.9g; Sodium 64mg

p76 Green Bananas and Yam in Coconut Milk Energy 122Kcal/504kJ; Protein 1.8g; Carbohydrate 3.7g, of which sugars 3.3g; Fat 11.2g, of which saturates 4g; Cholesterol 13mg; Calcium 47mg; Fibre 2.2g; Sodium 98mg

p80 Fruits of the Tropics Salad Energy 154Kcal/658kJ; Protein 1.3g; Carbohydrate 39.0g, of which sugars 38.1g; Fat 0.4g, of which saturates 0.1g; Cholesterol 0mg; Calcium 31mg; Fibre 4.1g; Sodium 40mg

p81 Coconut Ice Cream Energy 253Kcal/1065kJ; Protein 8.6g; Carbohydrate 34.5g, of which sugars 34.5g; Fat 9.9g, of which saturates 6.2g; Cholesterol 35mg; Calcium 305mg; Fibre 0g; Sodium 220mg

p82 Tapioca Pudding Energy 190Kcal/ 799kJ; Protein 6.1g; Carbohydrate 25.2g, of which sugars 13.8g; Fat 7.9g, of which saturates 3.7g; Cholesterol 18mg; Calcium 156mg; Fibre 0.2g; Sodium 70mg

p83 Fried Bananas with Sugar and Rum Energy 290Kcal/1213kJ; Protein 1.3g; Carbohydrate 36.4g, of which sugars 34.1g; Fat 13.7g, of which saturates 8.6g; Cholesterol 35mg; Calcium 10mg; Fibre 1.1g; Sodium 100mg

p84 Caribbean Spiced Rice Pudding Energy 304Kcal/1288kJ; Protein 8.6g; Carbohydrate 53.9g, of which sugars 37.4g; Fat 7.6g, of which saturates 4.5g; Cholesterol 20mg; Calcium 266mg; Fibre 0.4g; Sodium 110mg

p85 Jamaican Fruit Trifle Energy 400Kcal/1664kJ; Protein 2.2g; Carbohydrate 29.1g, of which sugars 28.9g; Fat 30.4g, of which saturates 19.4g; Cholesterol 80mg; Calcium 70mg; Fibre 3.9g; Sodium 20mg

p86 Caribbean Fruit and Rum Cake (per cake) Energy 10871Kcal/45678kJ; Protein 146.1g; Carbohydrate 1526.5g, of which sugars 1192.2g; Fat 448g, of which saturates 254.6g; Cholesterol 3.3g; Calcium 2987mg; Fibre 49.8g; Sodium 5.92g

p87 Apple and Cinnamon Crumble Cake (per cake) Energy 7217Kcal/30269kJ; Protein 89.9g; Carbohydrate 929.9g, of which sugars 500.3g; Fat 374.7g, of which saturates 233.7g; Cholesterol 1.7g; Calcium 2062mg; Fibre 34.1g; Sodium 4.22g

p88 Barbadian Coconut Sweet Bread (per cake) Energy 4078Kcal/17076kJ; Protein 59.2g; Carbohydrate 473.7g, of which sugars 154.2g; Fat 229.5g, of which saturates 156.9g; Cholesterol 609mg; Calcium 1373mg; Fibre 28.9g; Sodium 2.06g

p89 Duckanoo Energy 827Kcal/ 3499kJ; Protein 7.3g; Carbohydrate 161.4g, of which sugars 57.9g; Fat 21.5g, of which saturates 15g; Cholesterol 36mg; Calcium 224mg; Fibre 2.4g; Sodium 220mg

p90 Mojito Energy 226Kcal/941kJ; Protein 0g; Carbohydrate 15.8g, of which sugars 15.8g; Fat 0g, of which saturates 0g; Cholesterol 0mg; Calcium 2mg; Fibre 0g; Sodium 0mg

p90 Cubre Libre Energy 130Kcal/ 542kJ; Protein 0g; Carbohydrate 8.1g, of which sugars 8.1g; Fat 0g, of which saturates 0g; Cholesterol 0mg; Calcium 4mg; Fibre 0g; Sodium 0mg

p92 Demarara Rum Punch Energy 237Kcal/993kJ; Protein 1.4g; Carbohydrate 24.1g, of which sugars 24.1g; Fat 0.3g, of which saturates 0g; Cholesterol 0g; Calcium 20mg; Fibre 0mg; Sodium 10mg

p93 Caribbean Cream Stout Punch Energy 466Kcal/1950kJ; Protein 16.8g; Carbohydrate 37.7g, of which sugars 37.7g; Fat 17.9g, of which saturates 11.2g; Cholesterol 65mg; Calcium 556mg; Fibre 0g; Sodium 340mg

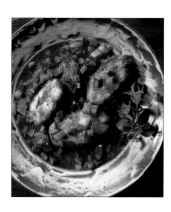

INDEX